THE SEARCH PRESS BOOK OF
DECORATIVE EFFECTS
FOR THE HOME

THE SEARCH PRESS BOOK OF
DECORATIVE EFFECTS
FOR THE HOME

LINDSEY DURRANT, SANDY BARNES,
JANE GORDON-SMITH,
MICHELLE POWELL & JUDY BALCHIN

SEARCH PRESS

CONTENTS

INTRODUCTION

Fashions change rapidly in home decoration and soon a room can look out-of-date. This book is a comprehensive guide to simple, practical, inexpensive solutions.

The following pages explore lots of the different possibilities for transforming your home – from applying antiquing effects and using decorative stamps, to painting on glass, ceramics and metal. Learn how to gild, stencil, crackle, distress, paint, stamp, sponge or lime a whole host of different items. The techniques are quick, simple, effective and fun, and skills can be mastered by everyone, regardless of artistic ability.

Colourful photographs and easy-to-follow step-by-step instructions will guide you through all the stages needed to master the techniques. You do not need to be an expert at drawing, as lots of patterns are provided. Nor do you need to be a designer – inspiration can be found in many different places: wallpaper, greetings cards, fabric, packaging, wrapping paper, posters, magazines and books are all useful starting points for designs. Keep your eyes open for unusual colour combinations and patterns. Just a tiny snippet from one of these could inspire you.

Although many techniques and projects are featured in this book, they are merely a catalyst to inform, inspire and help you on your way. The best results will often come quite by accident, so experiment, be creative and have fun. Whether you want to cheer up old furniture, introduce new colour to plain curtains or add a designer touch to your paintwork – let your imagination run wild. You will be astonished at the effects you can achieve.

PAINT
EFFECTS

LINDSEY DURRANT

There are many different paint effects, but I have concentrated on what I consider to be the main ones, including colourwashing, sponging, ragrolling, dragging and flogging. I have shared with you the basic rules for these but I hope that you will soon be experimenting to create your own variations. There are no rules that say you cannot use any household object to make a pattern in the glaze on your walls or furniture, so raid those cupboards and explore other possibilities.

I have also included a section on antiquing effects such as crackling, distressing, liming and gilding. All of these can be used on their own, or in conjunction with other antiquing or paint effects. You could even go completely over the top and use four effects on the same piece.

There is nothing mysterious or difficult about paint or antiquing effects, so have a go. Providing you follow a few simple rules, there is no limit to what you can create. Treasure found at a boot fair, objects in your child's bedroom, or the kitchen door that you have hated for years can all be transformed for very little outlay in time and money, to give you years of pleasure. For the purposes of this section, I have worked on small items, but you should not be frightened of applying these techniques to larger areas – doors, walls, floors or ceilings for example.

MATERIALS

You should not have a problem in obtaining any of the materials or equipment mentioned in this book. Everything is widely available from independent retailers and large DIY stores. You will also be surprised what you can utilize from your own home.

Paints

A neutral coloured vinyl silk emulsion or an acrylic eggshell paint is used as a basecoat for the paint effects. The paint effects themselves can be worked over the top using any water-based paint – from pure pigment powders to household emulsion or acrylics. All these types of paint are available in a fantastic array of colours, from subtle historic shades that will always be with us, to a range of bright contemporary colours that may come and go with fashion. There are also literally hundreds of shades of white to choose from. So, whatever your taste or mood there will be a colour that is right for you.

Brushes

You do not need all the brushes featured opposite to begin creating paint effects. It is best to buy the relevant ones as and when you need them.

1. Small paint brush   For painting small items and for detailing.

2. Medium paint brush   For basecoating or crackle glazing small to medium sized items. A brush up to 1cm (½in) will fit neatly into most small paint pots.

3. Large paint brush   For covering large areas, such as walls, table tops or doors.

4. Fitch brush   For creating a stippled effect. It can also be used for getting into awkward areas, and its chiselled edge is useful for straight, neat lines.

5. Stencil brush   A flat-ended brush for applying paint when stencilling.

6. Dragger brush   A long-haired brush that is pulled through the paint to create a pattern and leave an unbroken brushstroke.

7. Flogger brush   This is the longest of the brushes and is used to break up the surface of the paint. It is usually used in conjunction with a dragger.

8. Softener brush   A soft natural-haired brush used to soften harsh lines sometimes left behind in paint effects.

9. Bristle stipple brush   A square brush used for tapping the paint to give an all-over broken effect.

10. Plastic stipple brush   A cheaper variation of the bristle stipple brush. This brush will give a looser effect.

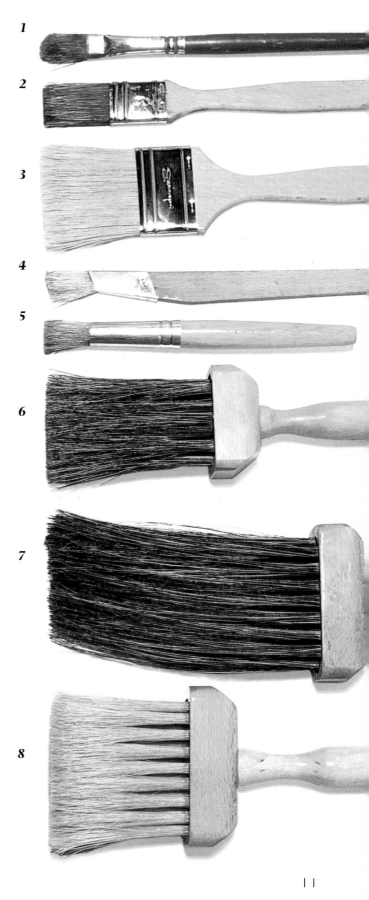

9

10

11

Other materials

The painting and antiquing techniques shown in this book all require different tools and materials. The essential ones are shown here. In addition, you will need a palette to mix the paint on – I use an old plate – or a paint kettle if you are mixing large quantities. A comprehensive list of all the materials you need accompanies each demonstration – you should check this carefully before you begin.

An ordinary paintbrush can be used for most of the techniques shown here. Where a specific brush is required, it is pictured.

You will need to use scumble glaze for all paint effects shown in this book, with the exception of woodwashing. Scumble glaze is a product which, when added to paint, holds the paint open (or wet) long enough to create a design in it. It also makes the paint translucent, allowing the basecoat to show through.

COLOURWASHING

Scumble is mixed with water-based paint for this and all the other techniques on this page. A softener brush can be used to soften the effect.

SPONGING

Natural sponges give the best effect, but you can use synthetic ones – try pulling out little pieces to create more texture.

WOODGRAINING

Rubber woodgraining tools are readily available. You can choose from a range of different sizes, which will produce varying widths of grain.

FROTTAGE

Clingfilm is used to create a frottage effect. You can also use newspaper – this will produce a more pronounced veined effect.

RAGROLLING

Lint-free cloths are used for ragrolling and ragging. Visit charity shops for old sheets to tear up.

LIMING

A bronze wire brush is used to raise the grain of wood. The wood can be coloured or stained if necessary, using a wood stain. Fine grade wire wool is used to apply liming wax or paste and a lint-free cloth is used to remove the excess.

CRACKLING

Two-part water-based crackle varnish creates the effect of aged, cracked varnish. The varnishes react with one another to form cracks. Oil-based paint or coloured wax is rubbed into the cracks with a cloth to reveal them.

Crackle glaze produces the effect of peeling, aged paint. It is sandwiched between two paints and it then cracks the surface of the topcoat to reveal the background colour.

Both of these effects should be sealed with an oil-based varnish.

STENCILLING

Acetate stencils are best to use, but you can use waxed paper ones. A stencilling brush or sponge can be used to apply the paint over the stencil.

DISTRESSING

White candle wax is used as a resist over a background. Coarse grade wire wool is used to rub back a topcoat to reveal the background.

GILDING

Dutch metal leaf is available in gold, silver and bronze. It comes in loose leaf or transfer form. Gilding size is a clear liquid that leaf adheres to. A soft brush is used to remove excess leaf.

PAINT EFFECTS

All the techniques in this section create a pattern in the paint, with the exception of woodwashing. The effects are worked while the scumble glaze and paint mixture is still wet. This mixture stays wet for quite a long time, so if you make a mistake you can simply brush through it and start again.

If you are working a large area, concentrate on only one square metre at a time, leaving a wet edge so that you can move on to the next section. If you are working on a large room, avoid ugly joining lines by trying to ensure that you finish a designated area in one painting session. For example, do not break off half way through painting a wall! To speed up the process, why not enlist the help of a partner. One of you can apply the scumble glaze/paint mixture and the other can follow behind creating the effect.

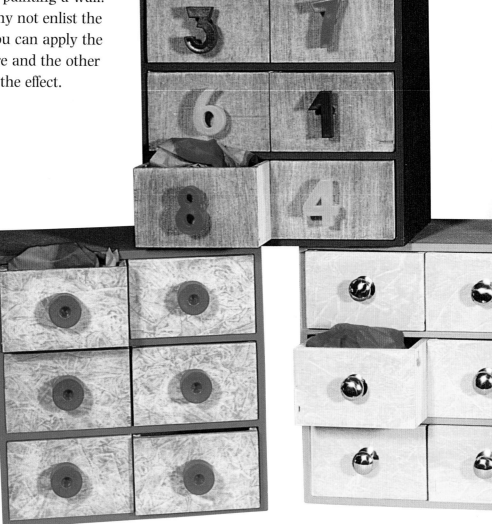

All these miniature chests of drawers are decorated using paint effects featured in this section.

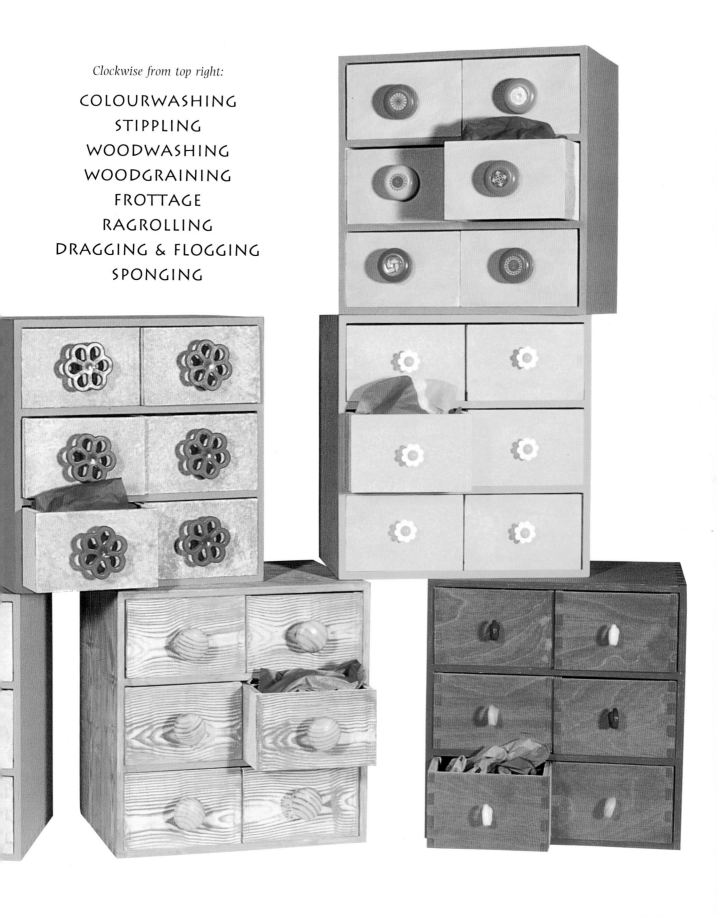

Clockwise from top right:

COLOURWASHING
STIPPLING
WOODWASHING
WOODGRAINING
FROTTAGE
RAGROLLING
DRAGGING & FLOGGING
SPONGING

PREPARING SURFACES

You need to follow a few simple guidelines before you begin working a paint effect. Preparation is essential and it is important that you ascertain what your surface is before you begin painting. Rough surfaces need to be sanded – there are various grades of sandpaper and wet-and-dry paper available. Primers are available for specific surfaces such as metal, tiles and formica. All surfaces will require a basecoat. I use vinyl silk emulsion or acrylic eggshell as matt paint restricts the movement of the scumble/paint mixture. I tend to use white or ivory for the basecoat colour as this shows up the translucency of the scumble/paint mixture best. However, you can use any colour, depending on your colour scheme and the effect you want to achieve.

Wood

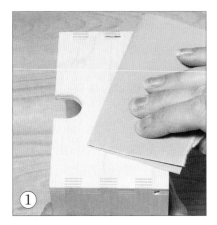

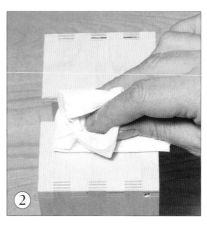

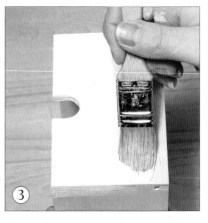

1. Sand the wood using a coarse grade sandpaper to begin with, working to medium, then fine.

2. Wipe over with a piece of damp cloth or absorbent paper to remove all traces of dust and debris.

3. Apply a neutral basecoat. It is best to use vinyl silk emulsion or acrylic eggshell. When dry, apply a second coat. Leave to dry thoroughly.

Plaster

Wash with warm soapy water to remove dirt and grease. Apply two coats of vinyl silk emulsion or acrylic eggshell.

Metal or ceramics

Sand with fine wet-and-dry paper to provide a key. Wipe over with a damp cloth to remove dust. Apply an oil-based or acrylic-based primer. Apply two coats of vinyl silk emulsion or acrylic eggshell.

NOTE

The information given here on surface preparation applies to paint effects only. Some of the antiquing effects require little or no preparation – instructions are given in each demonstration.

STARTING TO PAINT

Scumble glaze is mixed with paint to ensure that the paint will stay wet long enough for you to create your effect, and to hold the shape of the pattern. Mixing the paint with scumble will not change the colour itself, but it will change the intensity of the colour, making it translucent.

Pre-coloured glazes (colourwashes) are now available, but it is much more fun to mix your own. For small projects, mix the paint and scumble together on a plate. For larger projects, such as walls, mix in a paint kettle, an old plastic tub or a bucket.

> *NOTE*
>
> *The more scumble you add, the more translucent the paint mixture will be, and it will stay workable for longer. You can mix up to six parts scumble with one part paint – this will stay open for up to an hour. A 50/50 mixture will stay open for about thirty minutes.*

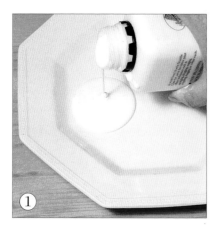

1. Pour one part scumble on to a plate.

2. Add one part water-based paint.

3. Mix the paint and scumble together using a brush. Continue mixing until you have a smooth, even colour.

COLOURWASHING

YOU WILL NEED

Vinyl silk emulsion or acrylic eggshell
Water-based paint
Scumble glaze
Palette or paint kettle
Paintbrush
Softener brush

①

②

Colourwashing leaves an all-over, uneven, random effect that is reminiscent of old painted plaster. You can either leave it with the brushmarks visible, or you can soften the brushmarks to create a smoother finish. This effect is particularly suitable for walls.

The size of the paintbrush needed will be dictated by the size of the surface you are working on (see page 11).

1. Prepare and basecoat your surface (see page 16). Apply the scumble/paint mixture loosely, using a random cross-hatch motion (see page 22).

2. Soften the effect by gently wafting over the painted area with a dry softener brush. Work the brush in various random directions until you get rid of the brushmarks.

NOTE

You can soften the background using a cloth instead of a brush if you prefer. This will create a more delicate, clouded effect.

Colourwashing lends itself to the earthy colours of the Mediterranean. Sand yellows, terracottas and rich oranges all work well with this technique.

WOODWASHING

YOU WILL NEED

Water-based paint
Water
Palette or paint kettle
Paintbrush
Medium grade sandpaper
Old cloth (or absorbent paper)

Woodwashing is a technique used to colour untreated wood. There are many ready-mixed woodwashes now available but you can easily mix your own. I use a mixture of water and good quality water-based paint to stain the wood. The wood should be coloured and not covered – excess paint is wiped away, to allow the grain to show through. For best results, choose a wood with a prominent grain.

NOTE

This technique does not use scumble glaze, and so the paint will dry quickly. Work small areas at a time.

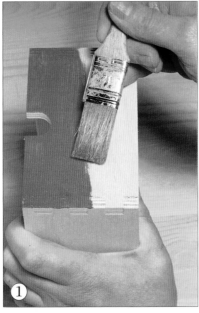

1. Sand your surface. Mix the water-based paint with water until it is the consistency of pouring cream. Apply the paint loosely.

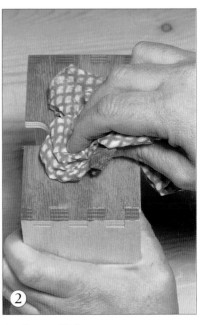

2. Wipe off the paint using a cloth or absorbent paper.

Woodwashing looks most effective on new, white wood with plenty of grain. However, there are many smooth-grained wooden items available which can also be transformed. Bright colours can look stunning, but for a more subtle effect, try using shades of off-white or cream.

SPONGING

The sponging technique has been around for quite some time, and it is an old favourite. In the past, the paint was mixed with water rather than scumble glaze and the result was a harsher, more rigid effect. Mixing the paint with scumble glaze gives a much softer, more translucent look.

This is a technique that looks particularly good when more than one colour is used on the same surface. Interest is added and depth is built up by randomly applying different colours as you sponge.

1. Prepare and basecoat your surface (see page 16). Apply the scumble/paint mixture loosely.

2. Pat a damp natural sponge on to the scumbled surface. Continue patting to remove a little of the scumble glaze and create a random patterned surface.

NOTE
The technique demonstrated here is sponging off. You can sponge on, by applying the scumble glaze/paint mixture to the sponge with a brush and then patting this on to your surface.

Sponging looks most effective in watery blues and sea greens. It is a great effect to use in the bathroom, or to brighten up a cloakroom.

RAGROLLING

YOU WILL NEED
Vinyl silk emulsion or acrylic eggshell
Water-based paint
Scumble glaze
Palette or paint kettle
Paintbrush
Lint-free rag

Ragrolling is a great technique that creates an instant effect. Most of us have got an old sheet lurking in the airing cupboard somewhere – there are no other special tools needed.

You need to change the rag frequently when working this effect, so it is a good idea to tear the sheet up into lots of pieces before you begin.

1. Prepare and basecoat your surface (see page 16). Apply the scumble/paint mixture loosely.

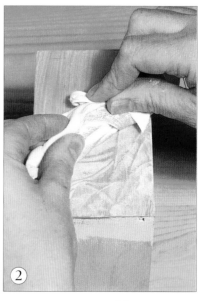

2. Form a rag roughly into a cylinder, then roll this over the paint. Continue, rearranging the rag as you roll, to produce a rippled effect.

NOTE

You can use a rag to make lots of different patterns. Form the rag into any shape that you like and dab it into the scumble/paint mixture to create different effects. This technique is known as ragging.

This effect looks great in any colour, and is suitable for any project, large or small. Try using it above a dado with a solid colour below.

STIPPLING

The tip of a stipple brush is used to create texture in this technique and produce a very subtle effect.

Stipple brushes come in lots of different sizes, and with different handles. It is often a matter of personal taste as to which you prefer. Plastic stipple brushes are also available – these are relatively inexpensive but still produce good results.

NOTE
You can stipple small areas with a stencil brush or add small areas of colour to a larger area, i.e. gold highlights.

1. Prepare and basecoat your surface (see page 16). Apply the scumble/paint mixture using random cross-hatching strokes.

2. Dab all over the painted surface with a stipple brush. Try to keep the brush vertical and stab it quite firmly into the scumble/paint mixture to create a soft texture.

Stippling can be used on pale colours to produce a subtle effect. A more pronounced patterning can be achieved if you work on darker colours. Stippling will create a textured, almost fabric-effect on walls.

DRAGGING AND FLOGGING

YOU WILL NEED

**Vinyl silk emulsion or
acrylic eggshell**
Water-based paint
Scumble glaze
Palette or paint kettle
Paintbrush
Dragging brush
Flogging brush

Dragging and flogging are,
technically, two different
techniques. Dragging looks
great on doors and flogging is
very effective on walls.
However, in this demonst-
ration, the techniques are
worked together rather than
separately.

1. Prepare and basecoat your
surface (see page 16). Apply the
scumble/paint mixture in a
downward motion.

2. Pull the dragging brush
down through the paint. Try to
keep the brush hairs as parallel
to the surface as possible.

*Dragging and
flogging looks
effective in any
colour, but if you
want to create a
textured wall-
paper effect, deep
tones look
particularly good.*

3. Slap and bounce the flogging
brush up the dragged line to
break up the effect.

WOODGRAINING

There are lots of different grainers available, from fine- to coarse-heart ones. Depending on which you use, you can create the impression of different woods, with wider or narrower grains.

This technique takes a little practice. The most important thing to remember when using this tool is to pull and, at intervals, rock it to create an authentic grained effect. Remember, if you make a mistake or if you are not happy with the effect you have created, simply brush over the paint and start again.

NOTE

Rocking the wood grainer as you pull it towards you, is what produces the knot pattern. In order to achieve a realistic, random effect, you should try to avoid rocking the grainer in the same place on an adjacent row.

1. Prepare and basecoat your surface (see page 16). Apply the scumble/paint mixture loosely.

2. Pull the grainer slowly through the paint. Work towards you.

3. After approximately 15cm (6in), rock the grainer towards you and then away from you as you pull it through the paint. Continue pulling and rocking until you have covered your surface. Work one row at a time.

This effect looks most authentic when worked in natural, wood colours, rather than in very vibrant shades – try giving plain kitchen cupboards a new lease of life. You can use this technique on any surface, but it can be difficult to achieve a realistic effect on very small areas.

FROTTAGE

Frottage was traditionally done with newspaper, but clingfilm can be used nowadays – this gives a more intricate effect and it is much cleaner than newspaper as it does not leave ink on your hands!

You can frottage using two shades of the same colour to create a marbled effect. When the first colour is dry, simply repeat the technique with a second colour.

Frottage looks great on smaller projects such as tabletops or door panels. One-colour frottage can be worked in any colour.

1. Prepare and basecoat your surface (see page 16). Apply the scumble/paint mixture loosely.

2. Lay a piece of clingfilm over the wet scumble glaze/paint mixture.

3. Smooth over the clingfilm with your hand to push paint into the creases. Try not to move the clingfilm or the pattern will change.

4. Peel off the clingfilm carefully to reveal the pattern.

ANTIQUING EFFECTS

You can make anything look old and well-loved using the quick and simple techniques covered in this section.

There are some wonderful products available that enable you to artificially age a surface. Paints and varnishes take years to deteriorate, but nowadays it is possible to create the same look easily and inexpensively, in just a few hours.

Generally, antiquing effects look most authentic on objects rather than on, say, walls. It is possible to combine different techniques – for example, découpage and crackle varnishing – to create an inspirational piece.

Try distressing your new furniture further by deliberately damaging it – you could use a hammer to create dents, or you could hit it with a bicycle chain to create random pockmarks.

You can use a small amount of varnish or scumble tinted with a little dark acrylic paint to create the impression of fly marks – simply load an old toothbrush with the tinted varnish or scumble, and run a knife over the bristles to create a fine spray over the surface.

Changing handles helps to alter the appearance of a piece. Use cotton reels, buttons, or perhaps some unusual finds from a bootfair.

All these miniature chests of drawers are decorated using antiquing techniques featured in this section.

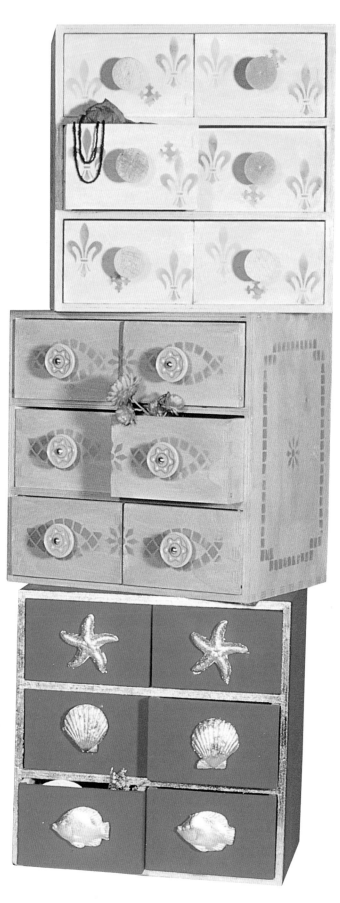

CRACKLE VARNISHING
LIMING
GILDING
VERDIGRIS
CRACKLE GLAZING
DISTRESSING

DISTRESSING

Cupboard

Distressing is a technique that involves rubbing back paint to give a worn look. To achieve a natural effect, it is best to rub back areas that would wear naturally – for example, around handles and along edges.

In theory, it is possible to distress any surface. This project is worked on natural wood which has been sanded first. The grain in the wood means that the surface is slightly raised in places; this will give a natural look to a distressed piece. I have aged the cupboard further by finishing with a tinted varnish.

Although this cupboard is distressed back to the bare wood, there is nothing to stop you from using a background colour, and distressing back to that.

I have used chilli and leaf stencils for this project, making it an ideal piece for a kitchen. However, you can decorate the cupboard using any image of your choice.

YOU WILL NEED
Small wooden cupboard
Emulsion paint: pale blue
Acrylic paint: red and green
Palette
White candle
Coarse grade wire wool
Chilli and leaf stencils
Masking tape
Stencil brush
Medium paintbrush
Absorbent paper
Tinted varnish

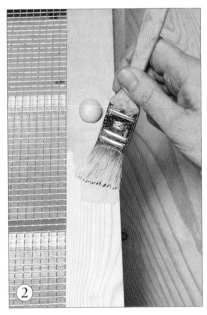

1. Lay a white candle on its side and rub it on to the areas you want to distress. Usually, the areas that would distress naturally are those that get the most wear.

2. Use a paintbrush to apply undiluted emulsion to cover the whole piece. Leave to dry.

3. Rub back the paint in the areas where the candle wax has been applied, using coarse grade wire wool. Work with the grain.

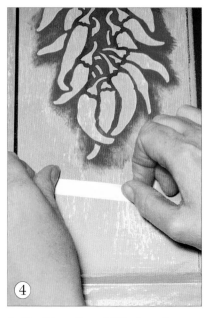

4. Position the chilli stencil on one of the sides of the cupboard, then secure it in place with masking tape.

5. Decant acrylic paint into a palette. Place a little paint on a stencil brush, then dab on to absorbent paper to remove excess paint. Work the brush over the stencil in a circular motion. Repeat, changing colours, to build up the image. Use the same technique to add a chilli image to the other side of the cupboard, and leaf decoration around the front edges. Leave to dry.

6. Brush tinted varnish all over the cupboard. Leave to dry.

NOTE

You can buy tinted varnish, or you can make your own by adding a little coloured acrylic paint to clear acrylic varnish. You can use whatever colour you like – choose something to complement your piece.

Distressed cupboard (see pages 28–29)
Distressing is an excellent way of making a new cupboard look old. Here, stencilling is also used on the cupboard to add interest, but découpage would be just as effective.

Opposite
Distressed variations

Distressing is the recipe for a perfect country kitchen. Use New England shades alongside natural wood tones to recreate an authentic farmhouse look.

Sewing box

There are lots of ways to embellish a distressed piece. Patchwork designs can be painted on and cotton reels can be used as handles to create an unusual sewing box to treasure for life.

LIMING

Spoon rack

Liming is a technique that can only be worked on wood. The lime is rubbed into the wood and it fills the grain to leave a subtle white sheen. You can use white emulsion instead of liming wax to achieve a similar effect. If you do this, you should stipple the paint into the grain using a very dry brush. The easiest way to achieve a dry brush is to remove excess paint on absorbent paper before you begin. Although this is a good alternative to liming with genuine wax, the effect will not be as authentic.

In normal conditions, you should have about forty minutes working time between applying the wax and having to remove it before it dries. If you are working on a large area such as a floor, for example, you may have to work sections at a time.

You can work on natural wood, or you can colour it first with a natural wood stain or a wood colour – the choice is yours.

To finish, I have worked furniture wax into this spoon rack to protect the surface further and to enhance the sheen.

You will need
Wooden spoon rack
Bronze wire brush
Medium paintbrush
Wood stain: antique pine effect
Liming wax
Natural furniture wax
Pieces of old cloth
Fine grade wire wool

NOTE
Woodstain gives a good contrast with liming. However, you can work liming wax directly on to natural bare wood. Alternatively, try woodwashing the surface (see page 19) to get a different effect.

1. Scrub over the surface of the wood with a bronze wire brush. This will raise the grain.

2. Apply wood stain all over the spoon rack. Leave to dry.

3. Work liming wax into the grain using fine grade wire wool. Work small areas at a time. When the spoon rack is completely covered, leave for approximately five minutes.

4. Use a cloth to wipe off all the excess liming wax, so that you are left with wax filling the grain.

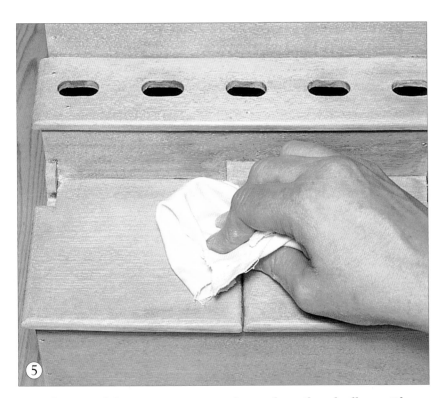

5. Rub natural furniture wax over the surface, then buff up with a clean cloth.

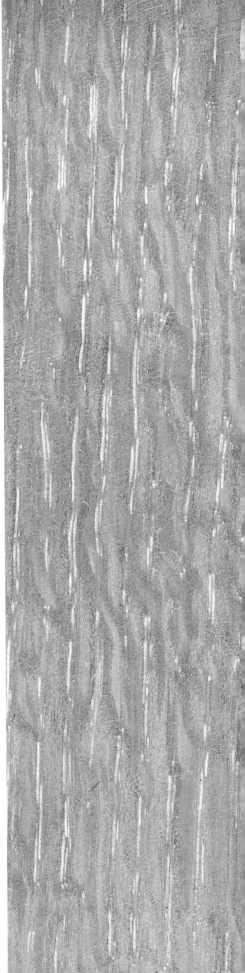

Spoon rack (see pages 32–33)

This piece is stained with an antique pine wood stain, before liming. The wood is fine-grained, which gives a very subtle effect.

Salt box

This wonderful salt box is made from a piece of old oak, which has a very open grain, and the hinge is made from an old piece of leather. It would be inappropriate to stain this piece, as the natural wood is so beautiful. The lime is therefore worked directly into the wood.

Miniature chest of drawers

Liming can be worked over a surface that has been coloured with woodwash. The addition of a stencilled design will quickly transform a simple piece of furniture into a mosaic treasure chest.

Opposite
Liming variations

You can lime any wooden item. Chairs, cupboards, wardrobes and floors can all be transformed. You can achieve a very different effect by colouring the piece before liming (see page 32), or you can stencil over the limed piece to add colour.

VERDIGRIS

Garden urn

Verdigris is the green and/or blueish effect produced by the oxidising of copper, brass or bronze. It has become very popular to emulate this effect and use it to decorate items such as candlesticks and garden ornaments.

This technique involves building up colour. A dark colour is laid down as the base, then two colours very close in tone are used to variegate the colour. If you are working on metal, you can use verdigris wax to colour the surface.

Gilt cream puts the finishing touches to the verdigris effect. It is worth keeping a brush specifically for gilt cream as it is difficult to wash out. If you prefer, you can use black patinating wax in place of the gilt cream to give a different effect.

I have used a cement urn for this project, but terracotta can also be used. Before you begin, wash the pot with warm soapy water and allow to dry.

YOU WILL NEED
Cement urn
Acrylic paint: dark green, light green, pale turquoise
Gilt cream
Palette
Absorbent paper
Fitch brush
Medium paintbrush
Damp cloth

1. Apply a coat of dark green acrylic paint all over the urn. Leave to dry.

2. Apply a little light green to a fitch brush, then dab on absorbent paper to remove excess paint. Randomly stipple on patches of light green.

3. Wipe off a little of the light green paint using a damp cloth. Try to wipe off from the raised areas, so that the darker green stays in the indentations.

4. Stipple on pale turquoise, using the technique described in step 2. Wipe off a little of the pale turquoise (see step 3).

5. Stipple on gilt cream to highlight the raised areas.

Opposite
Selection of verdigris variations

You can verdigris a variety of items, from elegant busts to plain terracotta pots. Even plastic urns, if primed properly, can be transformed into metal lookalikes.

Garden urn (see pages 36–37)

I liked this urn because of the Japanese design, which the verdigris highlights beautifully. The result is an impressive urn that will add a touch of class to any garden.

Miniature chest of drawers

A background colour can be used to complement a verdigris effect. I have used powdered filler over a stencil to create raised urn designs on this miniature chest of drawers. The stencil is removed and the filler is allowed to dry. The stencil is then placed back over the image and a verdigris effect is worked over the urns.

CRACKLE GLAZING

Key cupboard

Crackle glazing is a technique that creates the effect of old, peeling paint. A basecoat is applied and a specialist crackle glaze is painted over that. Finally, a top coat in a contrasting colour is applied. This top coat reacts with the crackle glaze making it contract and crack.

It is better to use a dark colour as a basecoat, and a lighter one as a topcoat. Some crackle glazes work better if the topcoat is watered down slightly – refer to the manufacturer's instructions.

Crackle glaze should be left until touch dry before applying the top coat – this will take approximately half an hour, depending on temperature and atmospheric conditions.

This project is worked on natural wood which has been sanded first. The cupboard is distressed as well as crackle glazed, to add to the aged feel. A coat of oil-based varnish or shellac seals the finish.

YOU WILL NEED

Wooden key cupboard
Emulsion paint: red and dark green
Palette
Crackle glaze
Medium paintbrush
White candle
Coarse grade wire wool
Shellac or clear oil-based varnish

1. Apply a coat of red paint all over the cupboard. Leave to dry.

2. Rub a white candle over the sides and top of the cupboard.

3. Apply a coat of dark green over the areas rubbed with the candle.

4. Rub back the green top coat with coarse grade wire wool.

5. Apply crackle glaze medium over the front of the painted cupboard. Leave until touch-dry.

6. Apply a topcoat of dark green over the area covered in crackle varnish. Leave to dry for the cracks to appear. Apply a coat of shellac or oil-based varnish.

NOTE
Paint the topcoat on quickly and do not go back and repaint areas as this will pull the paint off.

Key cupboard *(see pages 40–41)*
This key cupboard is crackle glazed and distressed to age it. An old key glued to the front of the door adds the finishing touch.

Miniature chest of drawers
You can be as over-the-top as you like with crackle glaze. It can be worked under simple découpage and handpainted images to create a very dramatic effect.

Opposite
Crackle glazed variations
Look out for old watering cans and buckets to transform using the crackle glazing technique. Stencilling can also be used to add a touch more colour.

CRACKLE VARNISHING

Jewellery box

Crackle varnishing allows you to produce fine, random, hairline cracks like those found on old masters, antique porcelain or aged varnished furniture. A colour is rubbed in to the cracks to reveal them. I have used a green, verdigris wax for this project, but you can use any coloured wax. Alternatively, use artist's oil paint, gilt cream or any other medium that is coloured, waxy and oil-based.

Water-based crackle varnish can be worked directly over card or paper, or it can used over a painted basecoat. Any water-based paint can be used as a basecoat – from poster paint or emulsion to acrylic paint.

Crackle varnish can be a little unpredictable, particularly in damp atmospheres, so be patient and persevere.

The border on this box is created using the découpage technique. Try to find a gift wrap that has a natural border pattern on it. Alternatively you can paint your own border.

YOU WILL NEED
MDF jewellery box
Two-part water-based crackle varnish
Water-based paint: cream
Palette
Verdigris wax
Medium paintbrush
Absorbent paper
PVA glue
Gift wrap
Scissors
Shellac or oil-based varnish

1. Apply a coat of water-based cream paint. Leave to dry. Apply a second coat.

2. Cut out strips of giftwrap. Mix up a 50/50 solution of PVA glue and water and brush on to the back of the strips. Stick in place to create borders around the top and the bottom of the front and sides of the box and the lid.

3. Apply a base coat of crackle varnish over the painted surface and the paper borders. Leave to dry. Apply a top coat of crackle varnish. Leave to dry until cracks appear.

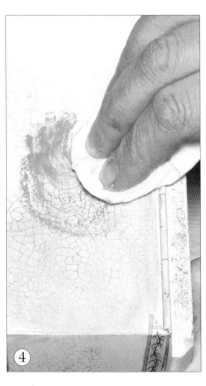

4. Rub verdigris wax into the cracks using absorbent paper.

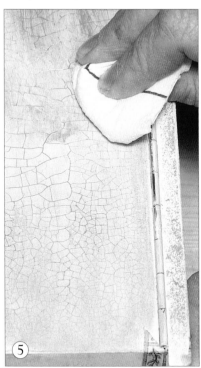

5. Use absorbent paper to wipe away excess wax and leave colour in the cracks. Leave to dry. Apply a coat of shellac or oil-based varnish.

> **NOTE**
> *If you find it difficult to remove the wax, you can use a small amount of white spirit on the absorbent paper.*

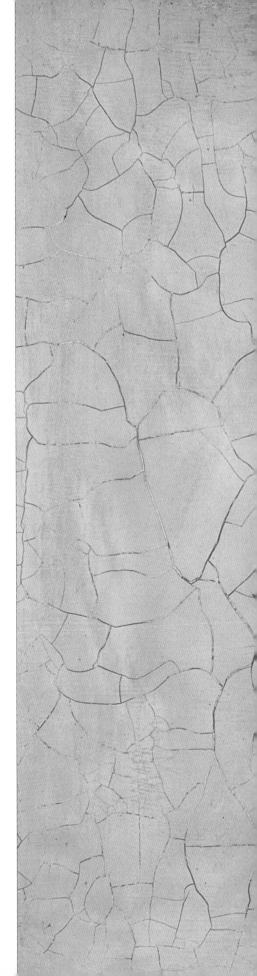

Jewellery box (see pages 44–45)

This box has been painted, découpaged and crackled. It started off life as a plain MDF box, which provided the perfect surface for a smooth finish.

(see pages 44–45)

Opposite
Crackle variations

The jewellery box featured in this photograph uses the same techniques as the project, but the cracks are highlighted with antique pine wax. Handpainted decoration on the lid complements the découpaged borders. You can combine techniques with crackling to produce fabulous effects. The orange table has dragged legs with a two-colour frottage and crackled top. You can crackle most surfaces, providing you prepare them correctly. The paper lampshade and ceramic lamp base both look very effective – particularly considering they were bought for next to nothing from a car boot sale.

Miniature chest of drawers

Crackle varnish is available in both small and large crack versions. I have used small cracks over stencilling on this miniature chest of drawers. Try using the larger cracks on a table top or wardrobe doors.

GILDING

Picture frame

Gilding is a quick and easy way to spectacularly transform a huge variety of items. It will add glitz and lustre to even the drabbest article.

Gilding is worked over a coloured basecoat. If you are working with gold or bronze leaf, try using terracotta or black underneath; if using silver, work over a deep blue.

Gilding looks best on three-dimensional objects such as plaster mouldings, wardrobe edgings, handles and door knobs. This project transforms a very basic wooden picture frame. I have used moulding to embellish the front. The amount of moulding you use will depend upon the size of the frame you are working on. You could use wooden or plaster moulding, but I have used a plastic one which comes with an adhesive strip on the back, so you do not need to use glue. This type of moulding is available from most DIY stores.

YOU WILL NEED
Wooden picture frame
Moulding
Emulsion paint: dark red
Dutch metal gold leaf
Gilding size
Small paintbrush
Soft stencil brush or soft make-up brush
Palette
Hacksaw
Fine grade wire wool

1. Use a hacksaw to cut strips of moulding to fit around your frame. Arrange them on the frame with ornate motifs for the corners. Remove the backing and stick in place.

2. Apply a coat of dark red emulsion paint all over the frame and the moulding. Scrub the brush into all the small areas to ensure that the entire frame is covered. Leave to dry.

3. Brush gilding size all over the painted frame. Leave to dry for approximately five minutes, or until the size goes clear.

4. Overlap small pieces of gold leaf on top of the gilding size. Work small areas at a time.

5. Tap the surface gently with a soft stencil brush to adhere the leaf to the size.

6. Use the stencil brush in a circular motion to brush away the excess leaf.

7. Gently rub the gilded frame with very fine wire wool to tarnish the surface slightly.

Picture frame (see pages 48–49)

This impressive gilded frame is very simple and inexpensive to create and it makes an ideal Christmas present or wedding gift. You can complete the project by adding a photograph or picture of your choice.

Miniature chest of drawers

I have used plaster shapes as the handles for this chest of drawers – these are available in craft shops. I wanted the gilding on this piece to remain really bright to complement the base colour. In order to achieve this, I decided not to tarnish the gold with wire wool.

Opposite
Gilded variations

You can use gilding to totally or partially decorate an item. Here, the firescreen and the cupboard are decorated with a gilded stencil image. To do this, the size is applied to the area inside the stencil, instead of paint, and the leaf adheres to that. The handles are also gilded on the cupboard to complete the transformation. You can gild anything – the vase is metal and the lamp base is pre-coloured ceramic.

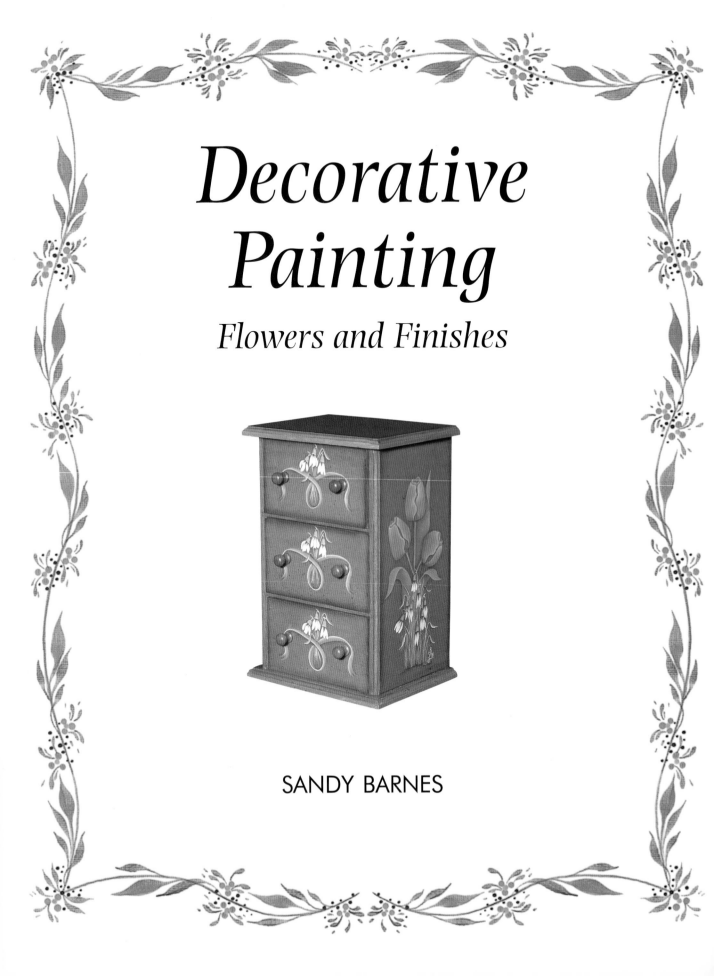

Decorative Painting

Flowers and Finishes

SANDY BARNES

Decorative painting is a general term used to encompass all forms of painting for decorative purposes. It is a huge umbrella that covers many decorative styles, but my particular interest is in realistic florals.

In this section, I do not go into detail about the various brushstrokes that are used in decorative painting – there are lots of wonderful folk art books which explain these clearly. Instead, I have concentrated on two techniques: side-loading and pat-blending. You will soon discover that both techniques are easy to master and are an excellent way of creating beautiful and realistic flowers and foliage.

I have also included examples of decorative background treatments, such as sponging, texturing, marbling and crackle finishing. I try to avoid painting a background in a single flat colour, as this can look quite uninspiring. Instead, I show you how to create interesting effects and textures which can then be over-decorated with flowers – in this way, pieces of furniture can be totally transformed.

The designs featured here are very versatile and can be used as shown or painted on your own individual pieces of furniture. If you prefer to create pictures to hang on the wall, simply paint the designs on pieces of MDF (medium density fibreboard), then frame them. Whatever your preference, I hope you enjoy painting these designs and will soon have the confidence to create your own.

Materials and equipment

Brushes

The selection of brushes available in art shops can be very confusing. It is worth investing in a good quality basic set of brushes – you cannot expect to achieve good results when using inferior ones. For decorative painting in general, choose synthetic brushes designed specifically for use with acrylic paint, as the hairs should snap back to their original shape when used. Most manufacturers now include a range recommended for decorative stroke work. Choose brushes with short handles.

If you look after your brushes carefully, they should last a long time. Always wash brushes thoroughly with pure soap immediately after use. Reshape while damp and allow to dry on a flat surface.

1. **Mop brush**   A soft brush used in the realistic marbling effect.

2. **Flat or wash brush**   The hairs taper to a sharp chisel edge. Choose a size where the length of the hairs is greater than the width – generally, a No. 6 or 8.

3. **Liner brush**   A thin brush with a very fine point. It is available in various lengths. Choose one about 1.5cm (½in) long.

4. **Round brush**   The hairs taper to a good point from a full body. Choose a small size (a No. 1 or 2) and a medium size (a No. 4 or 5).

5. **Filbert brush**   This is similar to a flat brush but it does not have corners. Choose a No. 3 or 4.

6. **Basecoating brush**   Choose a 2.5cm (1in) basecoating brush for good coverage.

7. **Stipple brush**   A small, round bristle brush. It is available in various lengths. Choose one about 0.5cm (¼in) long.

> **Note**
>
> When loading a brush with paint, try not to allow the paint to enter the metal ferrule of the brush.
>
> Never leave brushes standing in water, and do not allow paint to dry on brushes.

Paints

I have used acrylic paint for all the projects in this book. Acrylic paint is non-toxic, water-soluble, quick-drying and it provides a hard-wearing surface. It can be used thickly to imitate the appearance of oil paint, or it can be thinned with water and used as a watercolour. Although acrylic paint dries to provide a very resilient finish, you can varnish or wax your work to give an even tougher surface; this will also enhance the colours.

There are many brands of acrylic paint available, and there is a wide choice of colour. I have included a colour conversion chart at the end of the book for the paints I have used. Each brand of acrylic paint varies in consistency, colour-fastness, degree of coverage and price. To start with, I would recommend a make specifically designed for decorative painting. Remember that the quality of a paint is usually reflected in the price, so choose the best quality that you can afford.

Other materials and equipment

Once you have selected your brushes and paints, you will need a few other basic supplies . . . and then you will be ready to begin decorative painting.

1. **Hairdryer** This is used to speed up the drying of acrylic paint.

2. **Mediums** These can be added to acrylic paint to enhance or change its performance. A variety are available, including retarder (slows down the drying time) and extender (thins the viscosity).

3. **Fine water spray** You can use this to prevent your wet palette from drying out.

4. **Jar** This can be filled with water and used for rinsing brushes.

5. **Masking tape** This is used to secure tracing and transfer paper into position. It can also be used to mask off areas when basecoating.

6. **Absorbent paper** This is used to blot off excess water from brushes.

7. **Pure soap** Wash brushes in pure soap after use.

8. **Ceramic tile** A tile provides an ideal surface to work on when loading and blending paint into brushes.

9. **Palette knife** You can mix paints together using this.

10. **Wet palette** Decanted paint should be stored in a wet palette.

11. **Ruler** Use a ruler, thinned paint and an ink nib to draw straight lines.

The basic materials and equipment needed to begin decorative painting.

12. Compass with ink nib These can be used with thinned paint to draw curved lines.

13. Stylus This is used for tracing around a pattern when transferring a design. It can also be used to apply dots of paint.

14. Pencil A soft pencil or a felt-tip pen can be used to trace a design on to tracing paper.

15. Eraser Transfer lines can be removed with an eraser.

16. Coarse and fine sponge Paint can be applied with either a coarse or fine sponge (or both) to create a background.

17. Sandpaper Wooden surfaces should be sanded prior to painting.

18. White transfer paper This is used to transfer a design on to a dark background.

19. Black transfer paper This is used to transfer a design on to a light background.

20. Tracing paper Designs can be traced and then transferred on to your painting surface.

Suitable surfaces

There is an expression that decorative painters use: 'if it stands still long enough, paint it.' Provided you prepare the surface correctly (see page 60), you can paint on anything. I prefer to use wood or metal as a base for my designs. Furniture is ideal (either new or second-hand), or ready-made blanks like those shown below. Ready-made blanks are available from craft suppliers, and you will find an endless source of second-hand furniture in junk shops or at car boot sales crying out to be transformed.

Examples of items suitable for decoration.

Getting started

Your workspace

Light is essential for painting. Try to work in an area where you have a good source of natural light, or alternatively you can use a daylight electric light bulb.

Arrange your workspace in an orderly manner. Place the item you will be decorating in front of you. If you are right-handed, place any equipment that you will be using frequently (water jar, absorbent paper, palette, paints, brushes and tile) to your right; if you are left-handed, place these items to your left. Setting up in this way will prevent you from having to constantly reach across your piece as you are working. Items which you require less frequently can be placed on the other side.

Mixing the paints

Some of the projects in this book involve using colours obtained by mixing two or more paints together. For example, a peach colour might be made by mixing three parts warm white with one part red earth. Throughout this book, if a colour is obtained by mixing it will appear, for example, as: peach (warm white + red earth, 3:1).

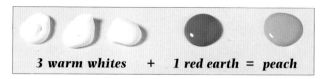

3 warm whites   +   1 red earth   =   peach

1. Squeeze the paint on to a mixing palette. I have used a ceramic tile for a palette, but you can use tin foil or waxed paper if you prefer.

2. Mix the colours together using a palette knife.

3. Continue mixing until you have a smooth, even colour. This mixture can now be transferred to your wet palette (see opposite).

Keeping paints fresh

Acrylic paints dry quickly once decanted from their tubes or jars and exposed to air. However, this drying process can be slowed down if the pools of paint are stored in an airtight container. Paints stored in this way can be kept useable for weeks.

Various brands of wet palette are available in art shops, but you can easily make your own.

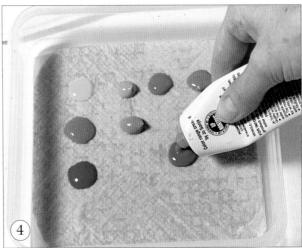

1. Spray a piece of absorbent paper with water.

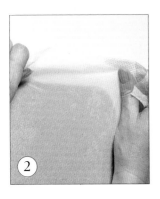

2. Cut a flat sponge to fit into the base of your container. Dampen the sponge, then stretch the damp absorbent paper over it.

3. Wrap the edges of the absorbent paper underneath the sponge then place this parcel into an airtight plastic container.

4. Decant small pools of paint into the palette. Put the airtight lid back on the plastic container when the paints are not in use.

Note

Use distilled water rather then tap water when making up your wet palette. This will prevent bacteria from forming and so will keep the wet palette fresher for longer.

The sponge must always be kept damp. If it begins to dry out between painting sessions, spray with a little water.

If a skin forms over the pools of paint, spray the inside of the lid with water, close the palette and leave overnight. The pools of paint will absorb the moisture, and the skin will disappear.

Surface preparation

The surface preparation of an item you wish to paint, is an unexciting but crucial stage. If you hurry or cut corners when preparing the surface, the finished piece will often be disappointing.

New wood   Fill any holes or cracks with wood filler. Rub over with medium grade sandpaper to remove any rough spots. If the surface is very rough, use coarse grade sandpaper to begin with. Finish off with fine grade sandpaper to leave a smooth surface. Wipe the surface with a damp sponge to remove any dust. The surface is now ready for basecoating. Some brands of acrylic paint contain a sealer; others need to have sealer added to them to make them suitable for basecoating. Refer to the manufacturer's details before you begin. It is best to apply several thin coats of paint rather than one thick one. To do this, apply the first coat, then leave to dry. Sand lightly and remove any sanding dust with a damp cloth. Repeat to build up several coats of paint.

Old wood   If the surface is in poor condition it is best to strip it back to bare wood and then proceed as for new wood. Use a commercial stripper and refer to the manufacturer's instructions.

   If the surface is in good condition but you want to change the colour, you should first rub lightly over the entire surface using fine grade steel wool soaked in white spirit. This will remove old wax, grease and dirt. Work in a well ventilated area. Wipe over with a clean cloth to remove any residue. Mix up a 50/50 solution of vinegar and water. Apply this to a clean cloth and wipe down again – this will neutralise the surface. Leave to dry. Sand with fine grade sandpaper, then remove any sanding dust with a damp sponge. The surface can now be basecoated. Proceed in the same way as described for new wood.

New metal   Most new metal comes with a rust-protective film of oil. Remove this with soap and water, then wipe down with a 50/50 solution of vinegar and water. Dry thoroughly for at least twenty-four hours, or in a warm oven. Apply a coat of metal primer, following the manufacturer's instructions. Sand with fine grade sandpaper then remove any sanding dust with a damp sponge. The metal is now ready for basecoating. Proceed in the same way as described for new wood.

Old metal   Remove old, flaking paint with a paint stripper, following the manufacturer's instructions. Use a wire brush to remove any rust, and to reveal the shiny metal. If the item is very rusty, use a commercial rust treatment, following the manufacturer's instructions. Now apply a coat of metal primer and proceed in the same way as described for new metal.

Above and opposite
Both the trug and the picture frame are painted on a sponged background (see pages 62–65). They are then decorated with honeysuckle and dog roses using the side-loading technique (see pages 72–95).

61

Decorative backgrounds

In this chapter I illustrate how to paint decorative and textured backgrounds that will enhance your painted designs. If you are painting a large piece of furniture for example, you may not want to decorate it with lots of flowers; on the other hand, a flat basecoat could look rather plain on the non-decorated areas. This is where a decorative background is ideal. Dramatic backgrounds can be created with the use of strongly contrasting colours, or subtle shades can be used to produce a more understated effect.

The examples in this chapter are designed to give your project added interest. You can sponge, crackle, texture or marble your surface to complement the painted design. All the techniques are simple and extremely effective.

Sponging ~ *simple sponging*

Gather together a selection of natural and synthetic sponges with different surface textures. Experiment to see which leaves the best imprint, by applying paint and then dabbing on to paper. Some of the synthetic sponges are rather smooth, but you can pinch off small pieces from the surface to create a more interesting print. My favourite sponges are the natural sea sponges. These produce a wonderful effect and, although they tend to be expensive to buy, they will last a long time if properly cared for. Never squeeze a natural sponge when dry; soften it in water first, and always handle it with care. Both natural and synthetic sponges should always be rinsed well immediately after use.

The sponging demonstration opposite consists of five stages. However, you can create a very simple sponged effect by simply following stages 1–3. Extra layers of sponging (stages 4 and 5) will add more depth and interest.

For this technique, you should mix retarder in with the paint that you are using for the topcoat. Retarder slows down the drying time, allowing you more time to move the paint. Choose a topcoat in a contrasting colour to the basecoat.

The finished piece
This background is easy to create using the simple sponging technique.

You will need

- retarder
- acrylic paint: red earth; teal green; warm white
- 2.5cm (1in) basecoating brush
- natural sponges: 1 coarse and 1 fine
- absorbent paper

Colour mixing recipes

• LIGHT TEAL

  teal green + warm white (1:3)

• VERY LIGHT TEAL

  teal green + warm white (1:4)

1. Basecoat your surface in red earth (see page 60). Leave to dry.

2. Mix light teal with a little retarder. Apply a fairly thin topcoat over the basecoat. Do not worry if the brushstrokes show.

3. Press a damp coarse sponge on to the wet topcoat. Vary the pressure to remove areas of paint and expose the basecoat colour in parts. Leave to dry.

4. Dab a fine sponge on to your palette and pick up some light teal. Remove the excess paint on a piece of absorbent paper. Sponge over the surface to transfer paint back over the topcoat. Repeat with a coarse sponge. Try to cover some areas more than others. Leave to dry.

5. Sparingly sponge very light teal over the board using a coarse sponge. Bounce the sponge on to the surface to soften the pattern. Add a little more colour in certain areas to avoid a flat effect.

Sponging ~ *multicoloured sponging*

You will need

- acrylic paint: red earth; teal green; yellow oxide; warm white
- retarder
- 2.5cm (1in) basecoating brush
- natural sponges: 1 coarse and 1 fine
- absorbent paper

Colour mixing recipes

• LIGHT TEAL

teal green + warm white (1:3)

When you are confident about using the simple sponging technique (see page 63), experiment with applying additional colours in patches and blending them with the sponge. Incorporate colours into the background that you intend to use in the main design – this will help integrate the two elements and will create a more harmonious project.

Note

It is not necessary to wash the sponge every time you use a different colour, but you should wipe off excess paint on absorbent paper.

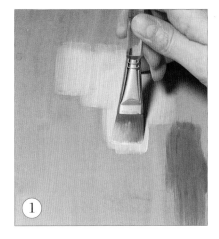

1. Follow steps 1 and 2 on page 63. Use a basecoating brush to add patches of yellow oxide, warm white and teal green while the light teal topcoat is still wet.

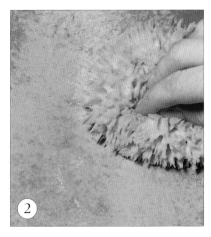

2. Use a coarse sponge to blend the edge of each colour patch. Wipe off excess colour on absorbent paper between sponging each patch. Sponge in between the colours to expose the background colour. Leave to dry.

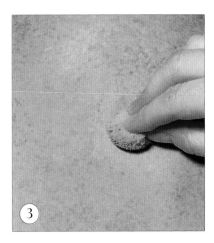

3. Use both a coarse and fine sponge to pat light teal over the entire surface. Bounce the sponges firmly to soften the effect. Reinforce the yellow, white and green areas with a little more colour. Continue sponging until the required effect is achieved. Leave to dry.

4. Use a fine and coarse sponge to add more colour. Slightly extend each patch, blending it into the neighbouring one while the paint is still wet. Clean the coarse sponge, and then bounce it over the whole surface to soften the effect.

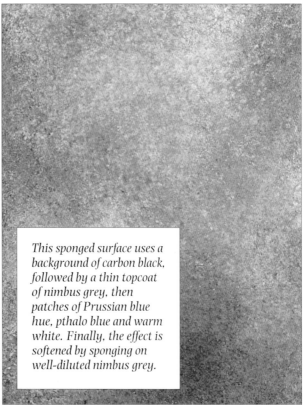

This sponged surface uses a background of carbon black, followed by a thin topcoat of nimbus grey, then patches of Prussian blue hue, pthalo blue and warm white. Finally, the effect is softened by sponging on well-diluted nimbus grey.

A dark background can be very effective when oversponged with pale colours. Here, a background of red earth is applied, then a thin topcoat of light grey (nimbus grey + warm white, 1:1) followed by patches of beige (fawn + warm white, 1:1), light yellow (yellow oxide + warm white, ½:1), cream (smoked pearl + warm white, 1:1) and light green (moss green + warm white, 1:1). Finally, the effect is softened by sponging on well-diluted warm white.

The finished piece
This gently gradated effect is created by sponging with several colours.

Texturing

Textured backgrounds can be achieved using a variety of everyday household items. Look for things that have a bumpy or uneven surface. These can be used to 'print' their pattern into the paint.

For this technique, as with sponging, two contrasting colours are used one on top of the other. When the textured surface is pressed on to the wet topcoat, some of the paint is removed, exposing the background colour. Remember, strongly contrasting colours produce a dramatic effect, while subtle contrasts will give a softer result.

The basic preparation is the same as for sponging (see page 63). You should basecoat your surface, and allow it to dry. Then, apply a thin topcoat which has a little retarder added to it, and proceed as shown in the examples on this page.

Note

Depending on how much water you add to your paint, a different effect will be achieved: a watery consistency will result in a soft, blurred pattern; a thicker consistency will give a sharper, more defined result. Experiment to see which effect you prefer.

Try using a bottle brush to add texture to your background. Press it into the wet topcoat with the flat of your hand. You can alter the angle of the brush to achieve a random pattern.

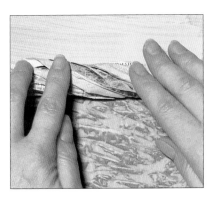

Newspaper can be used to create a striking pattern. Simply roll a length of twisted paper across the wet topcoat.

Bubble wrap can be laid over a wet topcoat and pressed evenly over the whole surface. In this example the pattern is very even. If a more random pattern is required, the bubble wrap can be reapplied at a slightly different angle, while the topcoat is still wet.

A simple plastic bag can make an effective texturing tool. Cut a square from the bag and then scrunch it up into a pad. Press the pad into the wet topcoat, and move it about to achieve a random pattern.

Try using absorbent paper to create a subtle pattern. Lay the paper over a wet topcoat and cover with a flat object, i.e. a book or a piece of wood. Press the flat object gently, then carefully remove it and the absorbent paper. For this technique it is important not to press the absorbent paper with your fingers or hand as this will leave an uneven imprint.

Cracklefinishing

You will need

- acrylic paint: red earth; opal
- crackle medium
- 2.5cm (1in) basecoating brush

This is a technique that results in new paint looking weathered and cracked as if it were aged paint. The effect is achieved by painting a layer of crackle medium (a sticky transparent substance) over a dry basecoated surface, and then applying a topcoat of paint. As the topcoat dries, the crackle medium causes it to crack, and the colour of the basecoat is revealed through these cracks. There are lots of different crackle mediums available; some will produce small cracks, some larger. The finished effect also depends on how thickly you apply the crackle medium. Experiment with different applications to see which effect you prefer.

Note

The consistency and thickness of the topcoat of paint will affect the size of the cracks. The thinner the paint mixture, the finer the cracks; the thicker the paint, the coarser the cracks.

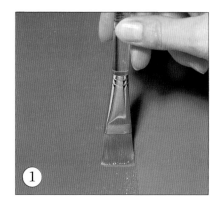

1. Basecoat your surface using red earth (see page 60). Leave to dry. Apply a layer of crackle medium. Do not overbrush. Any brush marks will even out during drying. Allow to dry at room temperature for approximately an hour until slightly tacky.

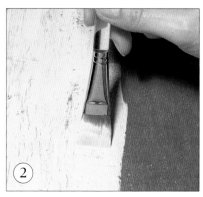

2. Apply a coat of opal. Do not overbrush once applied. Leave to dry at room temperature, preferably overnight, to allow the cracks to appear.

The finished piece
Crackle medium is an excellent and quick way of ageing a surface – and the result is very convincing. Here, a dark colour is used underneath a light topcoat to produce a good contrast and show the cracks clearly.

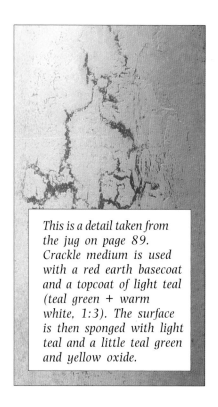

This is a detail taken from the jug on page 89. Crackle medium is used with a red earth basecoat and a topcoat of light teal (teal green + warm white, 1:3). The surface is then sponged with light teal and a little teal green and yellow oxide.

Quick and easy marbling

- acrylic paint: teal green; smoked pearl
- retarder
- 2.5cm (1in) basecoating brush
- cling film

Colour mixing recipes

• **LIGHT TEAL**
  teal green + smoked pearl (1:3)

You can have great fun with this easy but very effective technique. Experiment to produce different effects: use cling film for a fine veined effect, or a plastic bag for a coarser result; try using a dark colour over a light background, then a light colour over a dark one. If you are creating a background for a painted design, choose subtle colour contrasts to give a soft effect that will not compete with the design itself. Stronger contrasts can be used for an area that will not have additional decoration, such as the inside of a box.

1. Basecoat your surface using teal green (see page 60). Leave to dry. Apply a thin topcoat of light teal mixed with a little retarder.

2. Lay cling film over the wet topcoat. Use your fingers to push the cling film into creases, and form a random pattern.

3. Gently rub the flat of your hand across the cling film to force the wet paint into the creases. Be careful not to move the cling film as this will change the pattern.

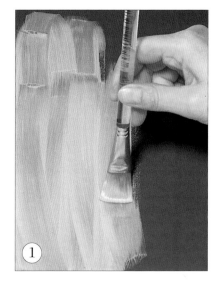

4. Carefully peel off the cling film. Leave to dry.

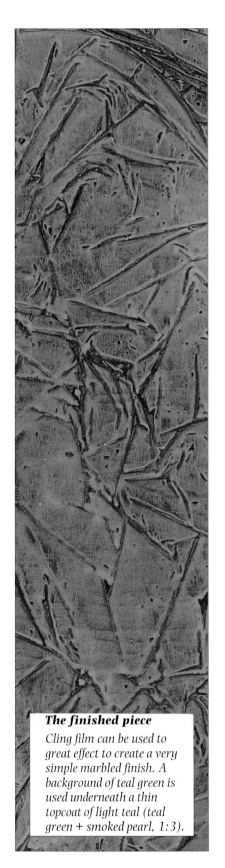

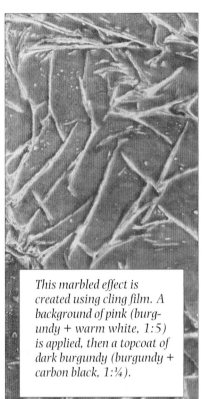

This marbled effect is created using cling film. A background of pink (burgundy + warm white, 1:5) is applied, then a topcoat of dark burgundy (burgundy + carbon black, 1:¼).

You can use a plastic bag for the marbling technique to create large veining. Moss green is used for the background, with a topcoat of light green (moss green + smoked pearl, 1:4).

The finished piece

Cling film can be used to great effect to create a very simple marbled finish. A background of teal green is used underneath a thin topcoat of light teal (teal green + smoked pearl, 1:3).

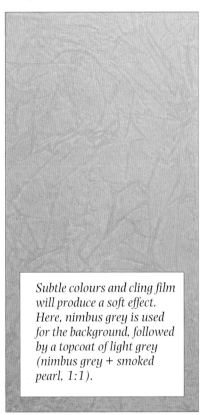

Subtle colours and cling film will produce a soft effect. Here, nimbus grey is used for the background, followed by a topcoat of light grey (nimbus grey + smoked pearl, 1:1).

This background is marbled using a plastic bag to create a more pronounced marbled effect. Turner's yellow is used under a topcoat of brown (raw umber + raw sienna, 1:½).

Realistic marbling

You will need

- acrylic paint: carbon black; nimbus grey; warm white; burgundy
- chalk pencil or watercolour crayon
- liner brush
- mop brush
- retarder
- 2.5cm (1in) basecoating brush
- natural sponges: 1 coarse, 1 fine

Colours mixing recipes

- **DARK BURGUNDY**
  burgundy + a touch of carbon black

Look at examples of real marble before you start this technique. In particular, study how the veins relate to one another, then make sketches of these vein patterns, which you can refer to.

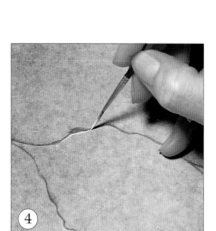

1. Use the multicoloured sponging technique (see page 64) to cover your surface. For this example, I have used a carbon black background then added a topcoat of nimbus grey, with patches of warm white and dark burgundy. Leave to dry, then mark in the veins with a chalk pencil or a watercolour crayon.

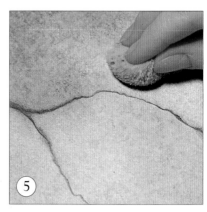

2. Use a liner brush to apply fine lines of dark burgundy mixed with a few drops of retarder. Work a short length at a time, painting slightly to one side of the chalk line so that it can be erased easily. Commence the lines using the tip of the brush, increasing the downward pressure now and again to create lines of varying thickness.

3. Every so often, stop and soften the lines with a mop brush while the paint is still wet. Use varying pressure when brushing the mop across the lines, to again create lines of an uneven thickness.

4. Add a few warm white highlights on one side of the dark lines using a liner brush. Paint short lengths at a time, blending with a mop brush away from the dark lines as you work.

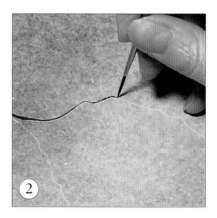

5. Reinforce and sharpen up the dark lines here and there using carbon black and a liner brush. Soften with a mop brush. Use a fine sponge to pick up more of the background colours and enhance areas close to the veins.

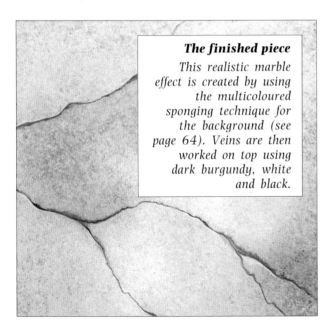

The finished piece
This realistic marble effect is created by using the multicoloured sponging technique for the background (see page 64). Veins are then worked on top using dark burgundy, white and black.

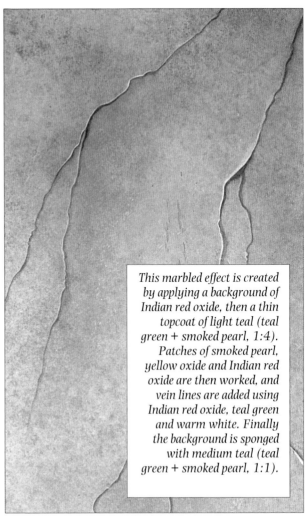

This marbled effect is created by applying a background of Indian red oxide, then a thin topcoat of light teal (teal green + smoked pearl, 1:4). Patches of smoked pearl, yellow oxide and Indian red oxide are then worked, and vein lines are added using Indian red oxide, teal green and warm white. Finally the background is sponged with medium teal (teal green + smoked pearl, 1:1).

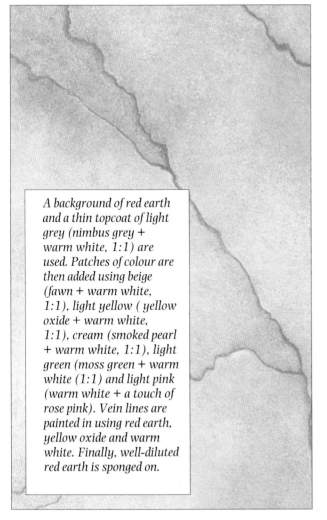

A background of red earth and a thin topcoat of light grey (nimbus grey + warm white, 1:1) are used. Patches of colour are then added using beige (fawn + warm white, 1:1), light yellow (yellow oxide + warm white, 1:1), cream (smoked pearl + warm white, 1:1), light green (moss green + warm white (1:1) and light pink (warm white + a touch of rose pink). Vein lines are painted in using red earth, yellow oxide and warm white. Finally, well-diluted red earth is sponged on.

This example has a background of red earth and a thin topcoat of light teal (teal green + warm white, 1:4). Patches of warm white, teal green and red earth are worked. Vein lines are added using red earth, teal green and warm white.

71

Side-loading technique

The side-loading technique involves working with a flat brush that has solid colour on one side, which gradually fades out to no colour on the other side. The process of blending paint across the brush can be greatly helped with the addition of a few drops of extender (sometimes referred to as flow medium) to the brush. Extender thins the viscosity of acrylic paint, enabling you to blend the paint across the brush more easily, and paint a longer stroke before running out of colour – once you have tried it, you will not want to paint without it!

I would suggest that you first practice this technique using a No. 8 flat brush, before trying a smaller No. 6 brush.

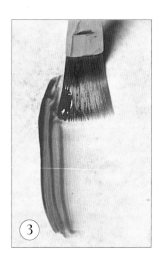

1. Pick up a little extender on a flat brush, and work it evenly into the bristles.

2. Dip a corner of the damp brush into a paint pool, to pick up a little paint.

3. Stroke the brush backwards and forwards along a 4cm (1½in) strip on a ceramic tile or blending palette. Apply slight downward pressure to the hairs of the brush on each stroke. Work in the same spot and use both sides of the brush to avoid paint building up on the top edge. Keep blending in this way until you can see that paint has spread three-quarters of the way across the brush.

4. Apply the brush to your painting surface. Keep the whole width of the brush in contact with the surface as you stroke the colour on, applying slight downward pressure. The finished effect should be a gradated colour with a sharp edge on one side, fading gradually to no colour at all.

Note

You may need to pick up more paint as you blend the paint across the brush. If you do, keep the clean side of your brush out of the paint.

If the brush feels as if it is dragging, pick up a drop of extender on the clean corner of the brush and continue to blend.

Water can be used instead of extender for this technique, but it is not as easy to use.

Photograph album

This album features an Australian flower design of flannel flowers, bottle brush and wattle blossom. Turner's yellow is used for the background of the crackle finish, with a topcoat of raw umber. The surface is sponged with burnt sienna, raw umber, raw sienna, burgundy and rich gold. The lace border is painted using the side-loading technique.

Lace is a good way of practising your side-loading technique (see page 81).

Leaves

Most designs contain more leaves than flowers, but these are rarely the focal point of a design. You should not, therefore, paint leaves with very bright colours as you want them to enhance and frame the main design, not dominate it. If you are painting a cluster of leaves, try to avoid painting them all in exactly the same way: vary the colour, size and shape; overlap some leaves and curl the edges of others to create a more natural design.

Here, I have painted a very simple leaf shape, but any leaf can be painted using this technique. I have used a No. 8 flat brush unless otherwise specified.

Flat leaf

1. Basecoat the leaf shape using medium green. Leave to dry. Mark in the central vein line with a chalk pencil.

2. Side-load the flat brush with moss green and use this to add a highlight along the central vein. Make sure the sharp edge is touching the vein line. Add another highlight to the top edge of the leaf.

3. Use pine green to add shading to the other side of the central vein and along the bottom edge of the leaf.

4. Paint the smaller veins in moss green with the tip of a liner brush.

You will need

- acrylic paint: pine green; moss green; warm white
- No. 8 flat brush
- liner brush
- chalk pencil
- extender

Colour mixing recipes

- **MEDIUM GREEN**
  pine green + a touch of warm white

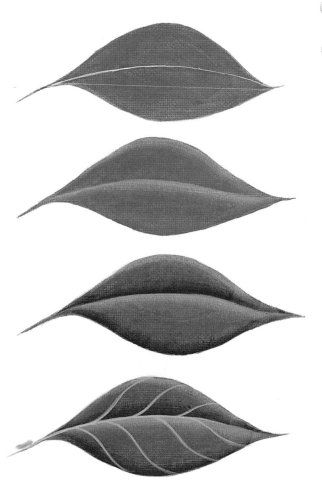

Curling leaf

1. Basecoat the leaf shape using medium green. Leave to dry, then mark in the central vein and the leaf turnover lines with a chalk pencil.

2. Add moss green highlights with a side-loaded flat brush.

3. Add shading using pine green. Note that the sharp edge of the shading should touch the sharp edge of the highlight.

4. Paint the veins in moss green with the tip of a liner brush.

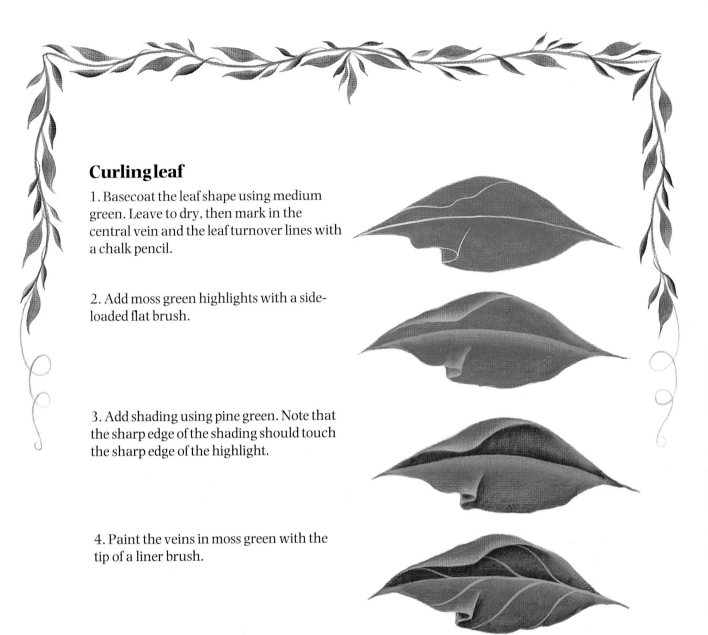

Note

When applying highlights and shading to create a three-dimensional effect, remember that the sharp edge of the highlight and the sharp edge of the shading should touch.

Flowers

Side-loading is a versatile technique that can be applied to all flowers to add depth and realism. The following demonstration shows how to create a three-dimensional flower from a flat basecoated shape, using the side-loading technique to add shading and highlights. Use a No. 8 flat brush unless otherwise specified.

This demonstration has been worked on a background marbled with a plastic bag (see pages 68–69). Nimbus grey was used as a basecoat, with light grey on top.

You will need

- acrylic paint: nimbus grey; warm white; Turner's yellow; burnt sienna; pine green; moss green
- extender
- plastic bag
- basecoating brush
- No. 8 flat brush
- liner brush
- stipple brush
- cocktail stick

Colour mixing recipes

- **LIGHT GREY**
  nimbus grey + warm white (1:1)
- **MEDIUM GREEN**
  pine green + a touch of warm white

The side-loading technique can be used to create a three-dimensional flower. Notice how the sharp edge of the shading and the sharp edge of the highlight are touching – this is what creates the three-dimensional effect.

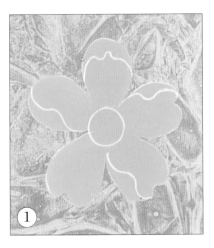

1. Basecoat the shape of the flower using Turner's yellow. Depending on the flower you are painting, apply the central lines and turnover petal lines using the method described on page 79.

2. Apply shading using the flat brush side-loaded with burnt sienna.

3. Highlight the curled petals in warm white using a side-loaded flat brush. Note that the sharp edge of white should touch the sharp edge of the shading.

4. Apply highlights to the edges of the other petals using warm white. Enhance the yellow centre with a further coat of Turner's yellow.

5. Apply shading to the bottom half of the centre circle using burnt sienna. Highlight the top half in warm white.

6. Use a cocktail stick and warm white to apply the dots for the stamen. This technique will create a dot with a hole in the centre, which gives a softer effect than a solid dot. Finally, apply a tiny amount of warm white to a dry stipple brush, and stroke the paint lightly on to the centre to add a highlight.

Pansies

The pansy is a nineteenth-century creation, developed from the wild flower *viola tricolor*. These multicoloured flowers were initially very popular with the Victorians but they have remained popular ever since. A huge variety of colour combinations and petal markings are available now, so there are plenty of pansies to choose from.

This project features the side-loading technique shown on page 72. The design looks equally good if you substitute or combine other colours, as shown on page 83.

Although the main flowers that feature in my designs are of a realistic nature, here, the additional flowers (referred to as 'fill-ins') are flowers that I have invented. I have used trumpet- and star-type fill-in flowers, but these could be substituted with any of the other fill-in flowers shown elsewhere in this book. You can buy brushes with blunt or sawn-off handles; if you have one of these, use it when painting the circle for the star flower in stage 5.

For this project, a No. 8 flat brush is used unless otherwise specified.

You will need

- acrylic paints: provincial beige; warm white; Turner's yellow; gold oxide; Norwegian orange; brown earth; carbon black; moss green; pine green; smoked pearl; aqua; yellow light; burnt sienna
- No. 8 flat brush
- No. 1 round brush
- liner brush
- stipple brush
- basecoating brush
- retarder
- extender
- cling film
- chalk pencil
- stylus
- masking tape
- transfer paper
- tracing paper
- soft pencil or felt-tip pen

Colour mixing recipes

- **LIGHT BEIGE**
  provincial beige + warm white (1:1)
- **MEDIUM GREEN**
  pine green + a touch of warm white
- **LIGHT YELLOW**
  Turner's yellow + warm white (1:1)
- **BROWN**
  brown earth + Norwegian orange (1:1)

Creating the background

Basecoat your surface using light beige (see page 60). Allow to dry then texture the surface using the quick and easy marbling method (see page 68) and provincial beige as the topcoat.

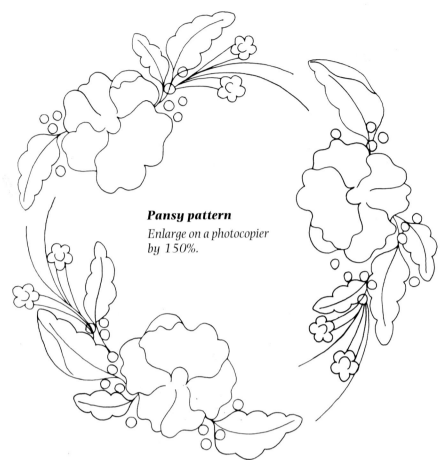

Pansy pattern
Enlarge on a photocopier by 150%.

Transferring the design

I have used a dark background for this project, so it is best to use white transfer paper; if you are using a light background colour, use dark transfer paper. The transfer line is a guide to follow when painting your design. After the painting has been completed, any remaining transfer line can easily be removed using an eraser.

Stage 1
1. Trace the outline of the design on to tracing paper.

Stage 2
2. Use masking tape to secure one edge of the traced design over the background, then insert transfer paper under the tracing. Go back over the outline of the design with a stylus.

Stage 3
3. Lift the paper to check that the design has been transferred.

Painting the design

Stage 1

Pansy: Apply a basecoat in Turner's yellow. Allow to dry. Reposition the tracing of the design over the flower. Insert transfer paper underneath the tracing, then use a stylus to re-trace the internal petal lines and transfer them back on to the painted flowers.

Leaves: Apply a basecoat in medium green. Leave to dry before transferring the internal lines over the painted image (see above).

Fill-in trumpet flower: Apply a basecoat in light yellow. Shade brown behind the petals, and at the base of the trumpet.

Stage 2

Pansy: Shade in gold oxide behind the petals and highlight in light yellow on the front tips of the petals.

Leaves: Use pine green to add shading, and moss green to add highlights.

Fill-in trumpet flower: Side-load a flat brush with Norwegian orange. Paint a C-stroke into the throat of the flower. To do this, imagine you are painting the letter 'C' with the sharp edge of the flat brush – keep the full width of the brush in contact with the surface as you work.

Stage 3

Pansy: Reinforce the shading in some areas using Norwegian orange, and highlight here and there with yellow light. Use a liner brush and Norwegian orange to paint the starburst from the centre outwards.

Leaves: Paint the veins in moss green using a liner brush.

Fill-in trumpet flower: Paint a C-stroke around the outside edge of each petal using warm white.

Stage 4

Pansy: Add liner brush work over the Norwegian orange starburst using brown earth. Work from the centre outwards, and use short strokes. Add a short fringe in warm white. Use carbon black and a side-loaded flat brush to paint a C-stroke into the throat of the flower. Extend the inside curve of the C-stroke using a liner brush and a few black lines.

Stage 5

Pansy: Sharpen up the shading using brown earth.

Leaves: Add more shadows on one side of the veins using pine green. Stipple on a little aqua here and there (see page 92). Paint in the central veins of the small fern-like leaves with a liner brush and medium green. Dab on tiny leaves along each side of these veins using a No. 1 round brush and medium green. Add warm white highlights.

Fill-in trumpet flower: Paint a strong highlight around the base of the throat in warm white. Add the stamen using a liner brush and brown earth and use yellow light and a stylus for the dots. Use a liner brush and Norwegian orange to reinforce the shading at the base of the trumpet.

Stage 6

Fill-in star flower: Add little clusters of star flowers around the design. Paint circles in Turner's yellow. Use the tip of a liner brush and warm white to paint short lines radiating out from each centre circle. Paint C-strokes in burnt sienna around the bottom half of each circle. Paint C-strokes in warm white around the top half of each circle.

Stage 7

Lace: Mark out the scallops with a chalk pencil. Use warm white to apply a side-loaded stroke inside each scallop with the sharp edge following the outside curve. Apply additional pattern lines with the tip of a liner brush, and use a stylus to apply dots.

Pansy hat box

The pansy design works well on a round object. For this hat box I used masking tape to mask off stripes around the outside of the box and the rim of the lid, and then I painted the unmasked areas in provincial beige. I used a No. 8 side-loaded flat brush and provincial beige to paint shadows along the sides of the darker stripes. The detail opposite shows how the delicate trumpet flowers are complemented by the pretty lace design. Notice the shading along the dark stripes around the box, which softens the harsh edges.

You can alter your colours to produce a stunning array of realistic pansies. The colours used for these five pansies are:

lilac pansy: lilac (dioxide purple + warm white, 1:2), dioxide purple, warm white and yellow light

pink pansy: pink (transparent magenta + warm white, 1:4), transparent magenta, Payne's grey, yellow light, carbon black and warm white

red pansy: napthol crimson, napthol red light, vermillion, yellow light, warm white and carbon black

pale blue pansy: blue (ultramarine + warm white, 1:4), ultramarine, pthalo blue, warm white and yellow light

purple pansy: dioxide purple, carbon black, warm white and yellow light

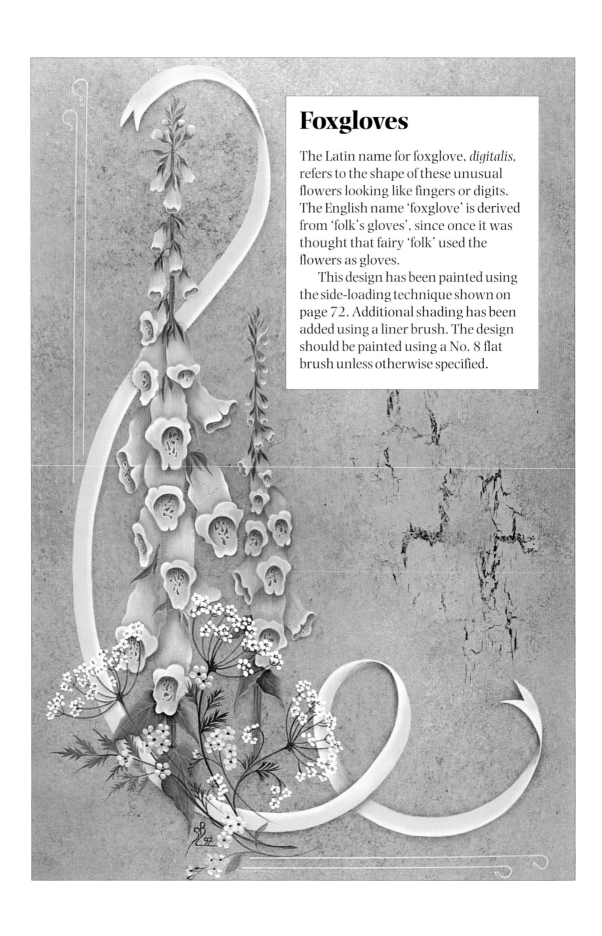

Foxgloves

The Latin name for foxglove, *digitalis*, refers to the shape of these unusual flowers looking like fingers or digits. The English name 'foxglove' is derived from 'folk's gloves', since once it was thought that fairy 'folk' used the flowers as gloves.

This design has been painted using the side-loading technique shown on page 72. Additional shading has been added using a liner brush. The design should be painted using a No. 8 flat brush unless otherwise specified.

You will need

- acrylic paint: burnt umber; opal; yellow light; yellow oxide; warm white; raw umber; smoked pearl; Norwegian orange; Turner's yellow; carbon black; brown earth; sapphire; jade
- No. 8 Flat brush
- No. 1 round brush
- liner brush
- basecoating brush
- crackle medium
- stylus
- transfer paper
- tracing paper
- masking tape
- soft pencil or felt-tip pen
- retarder
- extender
- natural sponges: 1 coarse, 1 fine
- absorbent paper

Colours mixing recipes

- **CREAM**

  yellow light + opal (1:4)

- **LIGHT PEACH**

  Norwegian orange + smoked pearl (1:6)

- **DARK PEACH**

  Norwegian orange + smoked pearl (1:2)

- **DARK GREEN**

  yellow light + carbon black (1:¼)

- **LIGHT GREEN**

  yellow light + a touch of carbon black

- **VERY LIGHT GREEN**

  light green + a touch of yellow light

- **LIGHT BLUE**

  saphire + warm white (1:3)

- **MEDIUM OLIVE**

  yellow light + smoked pearl + carbon black (1:2:¼)

- **LIGHT OLIVE**

  yellow light + smoked pearl (1:1) + a touch of carbon black

- **YELLOW**

  yellow oxide + smoked pearl (1:3)

Foxglove pattern
Enlarge on a photocopier by 200%.

Creating the background

Basecoat your surface using burnt umber (see page 60). Paint on patches of crackle medium here and there (see page 67), avoiding the area where the design will be painted. Use the multicoloured sponging technique shown on page 64 to apply a topcoat of medium olive. Add patches of light olive, jade and yellow. Finally, sponge into the background here and there using a small amount of light peach.

Leave to dry, then transfer the ribbon pattern on to the background (see page 79).

Painting the design

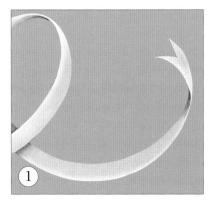

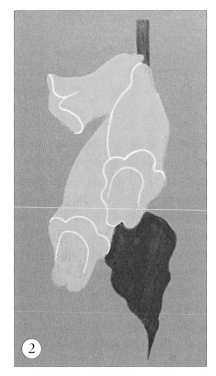

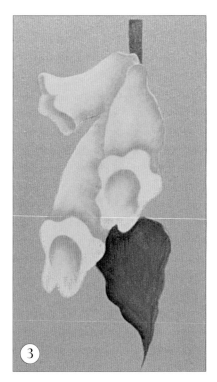

Stage 1

Ribbon: Apply a basecoat of cream. Highlight one edge of the ribbon in warm white. Remember that where the ribbon twists, the edge which is to be highlighted changes. Shade into the twist of the ribbon with raw umber. Use the tip of a liner brush to apply more shading and highlights. Work in very fine lines of varying lengths. Leave to dry, then transfer the rest of the foxglove design.

Stage 2

Foxgloves: Apply a basecoat of light peach. Leave to dry then transfer the internal petal lines on to the painted surface.

Leaves: Apply a basecoat of light green.

Stage 3

Foxgloves: Shade dark peach into the petals.

Leaves: Shade dark green into the leaves.

Stage 4

Foxgloves: Highlight the petals in warm white.

Leaves: Highlight the leaves in yellow light.

Stage 5

Foxglove: Hold a liner brush upright and use the very tip of it to add dark peach shading. Try to use very fine lines of varying lengths. Slightly extend the first layer of shading.

Leaves: Add more shading in dark green – use a liner brush and the same technique as for the foxglove shading to do this.

Stage 6

Foxglove: Use Norwegian orange and a liner brush to paint small irregular shapes into the throat of each flower. Leave to dry then outline these shapes in warm white.

Leaves: Use a liner brush and very light green to paint in the veins.

Stage 7

Foxglove: Shade into the throat with raw umber. Add more shading here and there using raw umber and a liner brush – use the same technique as in stage 5 to do this.

Leaves: Use a liner brush to paint a dark green line to one side of each of the light green veins – this will create shading.

4

5

6

7

Stage 8

Blue fill-in flowers: Pick up blobs of light blue and white together on the tip of a No. 1 round brush. Pat the brush on to the background to create clusters of petals. Leave a space in the centre of each cluster. Paint the stems in dark green.

White fill-in flowers: Use the same technique as for the blue fill-in flowers, but use warm white only. Paint the stems in dark green.

Stage 9

Blue fill-in flowers: Use a stylus to apply a dot of Turner's yellow to the centre of each flower. Paint the leaves in dark green.

White fill-in flowers: Apply a dot of brown earth to the centre of each flower using a stylus. Paint the leaves in dark green.

Stage 10

Blue fill-in flowers: Use a stylus to add a tiny dot of black to the centre of each flower.

White fill-in flowers: Use a stylus to add a tiny dot of yellow light to the centre of each flower.

Foxglove jug

Patches of crackle are worked over this enamel jug (see page 67), then the background is oversponged with light teal. When dry, a variation of the foxglove design shown in this project is painted on.

Door finger plate

You can simplify the foxglove design and work it on a smaller object. Here, the background is a flat coat of warm white, and the edging is worked with a side-loaded brush.

OPPOSITE
Umbrella stand

Here, I have adapted the design given in the project by extending the ribbon and including a small floral detail. Once you are confident with the basic techniques, you can customize designs to suit the shape of the item you are decorating.

Poppies

Poppies have long been a favourite subject for artists; the French artist, Monet, is particularly renowned for painting them.

This design has been painted mainly using the side-loading technique shown on page 72.

Additional shading and highlights have been added to the flowers using a liner brush, and sponging and stippling techniques have been used for the view.

You should use a No. 8 flat brush for this project unless otherwise specified.

You will need

- acrylic paint: teal green; napthol red light; brown earth; smoked pearl; Turner's yellow; warm white; Payne's grey; yellow light; brilliant green; raw umber; ultramarine; opal
- No. 8 flat brush
- No. 1 round brush
- liner brush
- stipple brush
- basecoating brush
- cocktail stick
- transfer paper
- masking tape
- stylus
- tracing paper
- soft pencil or felt-tip
- retarder
- extender
- natural sponge: 1 fine, 1 coarse
- absorbent paper

Colour mixing recipes

• LIGHT TEAL
teal green + smoked pearl (1:4)

• DARK RED
napthol red light + brown earth + smoked pearl (3:1:1)

• VERY DARK RED
dark red + a touch of Payne's grey

• MEDIUM RED
dark red + smoked pearl + Turner's yellow (1:$\frac{1}{3}$:$\frac{1}{2}$)

• LIGHT RED
medium red + warm white (1:$\frac{1}{2}$) + a touch of Turner's yellow

• DARK GREEN
brilliant green + smoked pearl + brown earth (2:2:3)

• MEDIUM GREEN
dark green + smoked pearl (1:1)

• LIGHT GREEN
medium green + a touch of yellow light

• VERY LIGHT GREEN
light green + a touch of warm white

• BLUE
ultramarine + warm white (1:4)

• LIGHT OPAL
opal + warm white (1:1)

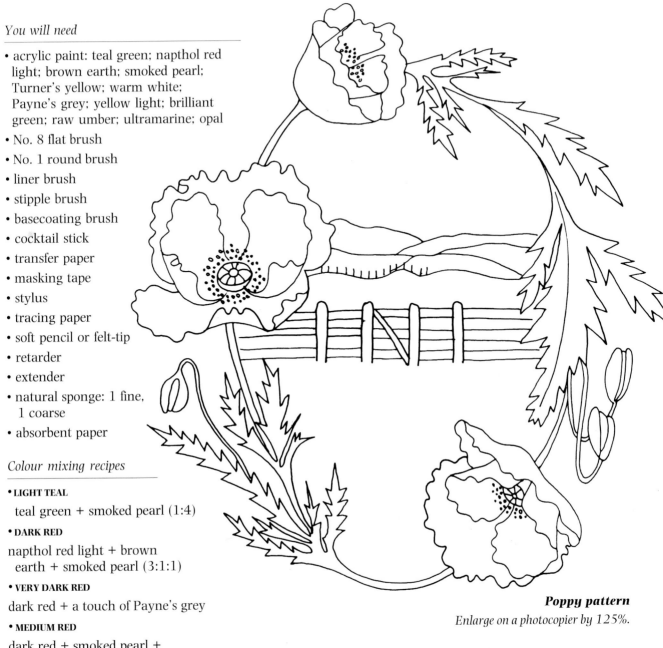

Poppy pattern
Enlarge on a photocopier by 125%.

Creating the background

Basecoat your surface using teal green (see page 60). Use the multicoloured sponging technique shown on page 64 to apply a topcoat of light teal, and then patches of smoked pearl and Turner's yellow. Leave to dry, then transfer the design on to the surface (see page 79).

Painting the design

Stage 1

View: Use a damp fine sponge to apply medium green over the fields and hills, and use blue over the sky area.

Leaves: Apply a basecoat of light green to the leaves and stems using a No. 1 round brush.

Poppies: Apply a basecoat of dark red to the petals. Leave to dry before transferring the internal petal lines on to the painted surface.

Stage 2

View: Paint the hill contours using a liner brush and dark green. Apply a basecoat of opal to the fence. Stipple in some indication of foliage along the hill contours and around the base of the fence using medium green. To do this, pick up a small amount of paint on a dry stipple brush, then dab the brush on to absorbent paper to remove most of the paint. Hold the brush upright, then bounce it up and down, depositing paint where required. Repeat, until the required effect is achieved.

Leaves: Paint in the central veins using a liner brush and very light green.

Poppies: Paint the flower centres in light green using a No. 1 round brush. Shade the petals with very dark red, then add highlights in light red.

Stage 3

View: Add shading to the fence using raw umber, then highlight with light opal. Paint the distant fence with a liner brush and raw umber. Highlight the sides of the posts with a liner brush and opal. Use a dry stipple brush and opal to indicate a worn path, then repeat with light opal. Stipple light and dark green here and there over the fields.

Leaves: Shade one side of the central veins in a medium green and highlight the other side in very light green.

Poppies: Add dark green shading to the flower centres, and use yellow light for highlighting. Use warm white to add more highlighting to the edges of the petals. Use the tip of a liner brush and yellow light to paint very fine lines on the petals; this will create highlights. Side-load a flat brush with napthol red light and apply this where the petals curl backwards and therefore are not highlighted on the edges. Create shading by adding very fine black lines made with a liner brush; these should radiate from the centre.

Stage 4

View: Use dark green to shade the background around the main fence. Paint tree trunks on the distant trees using a liner brush and raw umber, and stipple in additional foliage around the main fence. Use the tip of a cocktail stick to paint in white and red flowers in front of the fence. Use the tip of a liner brush to dot in poppies in the distant field. Paint clumps of grass along the path and around the main fence using a liner brush and dark green. Finally, stipple a few highlights in the grass and foliage using yellow light.

Leaves: Re-paint the central veins in a very light green using a liner brush. Shade around the outside of the leaves using teal green. Paint random spiky hairs along the stems and around the outside of the buds using a liner brush and dark green.

Poppies: Repeat the liner work in stage 3, to build up shading and highlights. Vary the length of the fine lines. Paint a black dot in the centre of two of the flowers. Use a liner brush to add short fine lines radiating out from the centres. Use a liner brush to paint the stamen, radiating from the outside edge of each flower centre. Apply small black spots of varying sizes over the stamen lines. Highlight one side of each black spot in warm white, using the tip of a liner brush. Finally, shade around the outside of the flowers in teal green.

Miniature poppy dresser

The poppy designs works well on this dresser. I added a short length of ribbon draped over the handles to decorate the drawer; this was painted using the technique shown on page 86, and medium red, with light red highlights and dark red shading. The edges of the dresser were shaded in teal green using a side-loaded flat brush.

Pat-blending technique

Pat-blending produces a similar result to that of side-loading and again, the colour is used over a flat background. The added advantage of this technique is that several colours can be blended together to create lovely effects.

In the example shown here, I have only used two colours to demonstrate this technique. It is best to experiment with two colours to start with, then apply additional colours as your confidence grows. This technique does require practice, so do not give up too easily.

Pat-blending is worked over a dry basecoat. Retarder is used under the topcoat to slow down the drying time of any paint applied on top of it; this allows you more time to blend paints together and get a smooth effect.

1. Apply a basecoat of ultra-marine. Allow to dry.

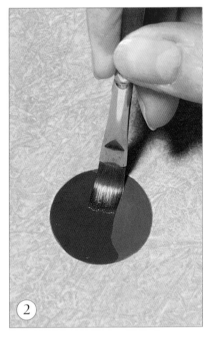

2. Evenly cover the basecoat with a thin coat of retarder. Wipe the brush on absorbent paper then stroke it back over the retarder to remove any excess. Continue until you have an even, shiny surface.

Note

Acrylic paint worked over retarder takes a long time to dry, so a hairdryer should be used. It is important to ensure that the first coat is thoroughly dry before applying the next layer of retarder; allow the surface to come back to room temperature before doing this.

Retarder will allow you to play with the paints applied over it for quite some time. However, it will gradually dry, and patches of paint may then start to lift off. If you find that your paint is not moving easily, stop and dry thoroughly with a hairdryer. When the surface is cool, reapply a layer of retarder and continue blending your paint as before.

Retarder should be applied sparingly. If you find that your paint is swimming around on the surface and not blending with the other colours, you have applied too much retarder. If this happens, wipe it off and start again.

3. Apply Payne's grey to one side of the circle with a dry filbert brush.

4. Wipe the brush on absorbent paper to remove excess paint.

5. Pull the colour in towards the centre.

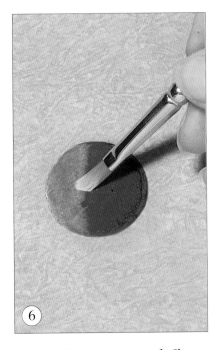

6. Turn the image around. Clean your brush then repeat stages 3-5 on the opposite side of the circle using warm white.

7. Wipe the brush to remove any excess paint. Now pat and blend the two colours down the centre so that they fade into the background. Keep wiping the excess paint off the brush during blending. Use a hairdryer to dry the paint and retarder. Repeat the stages shown here to build up more shading and to add further colours as required.

Leaves

The pat-blending technique allows you to build up additional colours. Try adding small amounts of colour into any leaves that are in the focal point of your design. If you want a leaf to appear in the distance or fade into the background, blend a little of the background colour into the edge of your leaf. This will also help to harmonise your design.

You should bear in mind the same points when painting leaves using the pat-blending technique, as when painting them using the side-loading technique (see page 74).

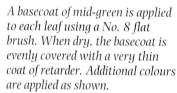

A basecoat of mid-green is applied to each leaf using a No. 8 flat brush. When dry, the basecoat is evenly covered with a very thin coat of retarder. Additional colours are applied as shown.

The patches of colour are blended by patting gently with a filbert brush. Where the patches of colour meet, they are faded into each other. The light and dark colours are kept well-defined down the central vein lines, and blended out away from the vein line into the rest of the leaf.

Flowers

You can use the pat-blending technique to paint flowers. This method will allow you to create wonderfully subtle shades and tones which will bring your flowers to life.

Tulips and snowdrops

Tulips were first cultivated in the Turkish court in the early sixteenth century. Fortunes were made in the European bulb trade during the seventeenth century, with single tulip bulbs fetching the equivalent of thousands of pounds. Tulips have featured in traditional folk art designs for hundreds of years, and they were originally painted to symbolise the Holy Trinity.

Snowdrops also feature in this design. These are sometimes referred to as 'purification flowers' as they are associated with the religious festival, Candlemas, which celebrates the Feast of the Purification of the Virgin Mary and the presentation of Christ in the Temple.

This design has been painted using the pat-blending technique shown on pages 96–97. The side-loading technique shown on page 72 has been used for the final stages of each flower. A filbert brush is used throughout unless otherwise specified.

I have worked this design on a subtle woodstained background. If you are not working on a wooden surface, use one of the decorative backgrounds featured on pages 62–71.

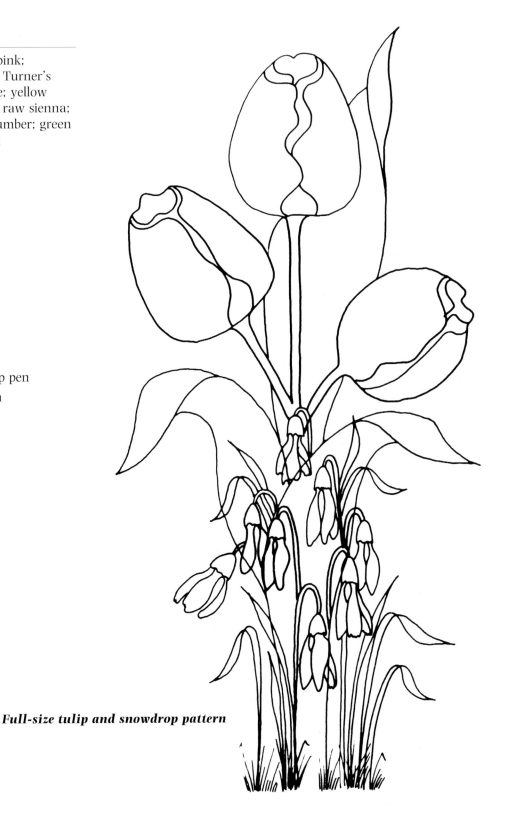

You will need

- acrylic paint: rose pink; Norwegian orange; Turner's yellow; warm white; yellow light; Payne's grey; raw sienna; burnt sienna; raw umber; green oxide; carbon black
- No. 8 flat brush
- No. 1 round brush
- basecoating brush
- liner brush
- filbert brush
- stipple brush
- retarder
- transfer paper
- masking tape
- tracing paper
- stylus
- soft pencil or felt-tip pen
- clear glaze medium
- dry cloth
- old toothbrush

Full-size tulip and snowdrop pattern

Colour mixing recipes

- **LIGHT PINK**

  Norwegian orange + rose pink + warm white
  (2:1:8)

- **DARK PINK**

  Norwegian orange + rose pink + warm white
  (2:1:1)

- **DARK ORANGE**

  Norwegian orange + a touch of Payne's grey

- **DARK GREEN**

  green oxide + Turner's yellow (1:1) + a touch of
  carbon black

- **VERY DARK GREEN**

  dark green + a touch of Payne's grey

- **MEDIUM GREEN**

  green oxide + Turner's yellow (1:1)

- **LIGHT GREEN**

  medium green + yellow light (1:1)

- **BROWN**

  raw sienna + burnt sienna + raw umber $(1:1:^1/_2)$

Creating the background

Apply a basecoat of neat clear glaze medium to
your surface using a basecoating brush. Allow to
dry. Make up a woodstain by using a 50/50 mixture
of brown paint with clear glaze medium; this will
produce a semi-transparent mixture which, when
applied to wood, will allow the grain to show
through. Brush this mixture on to your surface.
Remove brushmarks by wiping off any excess with
a dry cloth. Dip an old toothbrush in raw umber,
then flick the bristles to speckle the surface with
paint. Leave to dry, then transfer the design on to
the woodstained surface (see page 79).

Painting the design

Stage 1

Leaves: Use a No. 8
flat brush to apply a
medium green
basecoat.

Tulips: Apply a
basecoat using a
No. 8 flat brush and
dark pink. Allow to
dry. Transfer the
internal petal lines
on to the painted
surface.

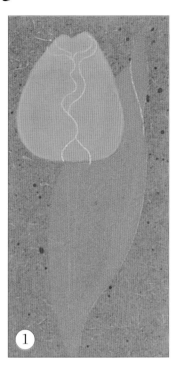

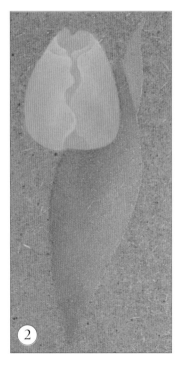

Stage 2

Leaves: Paint a thin
coat of retarder on
to the leaves. Apply
dark green shading
and light green
highlights, then
pat-blend these two
greens where they
meet. Allow to dry.

Tulips: Paint
retarder on to the
flowers. Pat-blend
light pink
highlights, working
outwards so that
the colour fades into
the background.
Allow to dry.

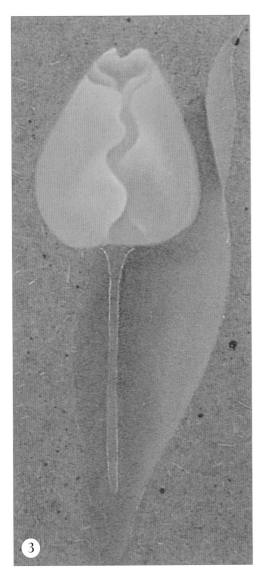

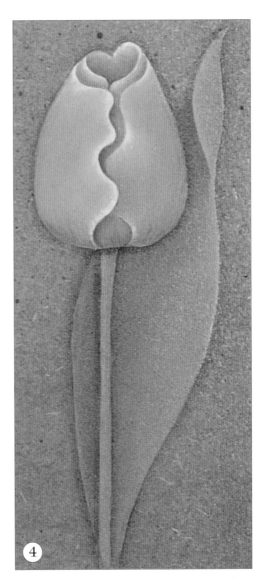

Stage 3

Leaves: Transfer the stalk lines on to the painted surface. Apply retarder to the leaves. Build up very dark green shading on each side of the stalks and under the curl of each leaf. Highlight the top of each leaf curl and leaf edge in light green. Allow to dry.

Tulips: Apply retarder to the flowers. Pat-blend on patches of rose pink, Norwegian orange and Turner's yellow as shading. Blend the colours well where they meet. Reinforce highlights here and there with warm white. Allow to dry, then repeat this stage if necessary, until the desired effect is achieved.

Stage 4

Leaves: Apply retarder to the leaves. Paint the stalks in medium green and pat-blend yellow light highlights down one side. Allow to dry. Shade down both sides of each stalk and under the leaf curls using a side-loaded No. 8 flat brush and very dark green. Shade raw umber around the outside of the leaves.

Tulips: Use the side-loading technique and warm white to enhance the highlights, and use dark orange for the shading inside the flowers. Add the green area at the base of the flowers with the tip of a liner brush. Vary the lengths of the strokes to give a gradated effect. Use a No. 8 flat brush and raw umber to shade around the outside of the flowers and under the base.

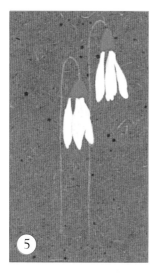   

Stage 5

Snowdrops: Use a No. 8 flat brush to apply a basecoat of warm white to the petals and medium green to the cups. Allow to dry.

Stage 6

Snowdrops: Apply retarder to the petals. Pat-blend medium green at the base of the petals, fading out half way down the petals. Allow to dry.

Stage 7

Snowdrops: Apply retarder to the petals and the cups. Pat-blend very dark green at the base of each petal and on one side of each cup. Pat-blend yellow light on the other side of each cup and along the bottom edge. Paint the leaves and stalks in medium green using a No. 1 round brush. Allow to dry. Apply retarder to the stalks, then pat blend on highlights using warm white. Allow to dry.

Stage 8

Snowdrops: Use the side-loading technique and Payne's grey to shade the base of the petals and in between each petal. Highlight along the bottom edge of each cup in yellow light using a No. 8 flat brush. Use a dry stipple brush and a little warm white to add the final highlights to the middle of the cups. Use a No. 8 flat brush and raw umber to shade around the outside of the leaves and flowers. Slightly extend the stalks using the same method as described in stage 7.

Grass: Paint in fine lines in the grass area using a liner brush and yellow light, warm white and all the shades of green to create variety and depth. Shade raw umber into the base of the grass.

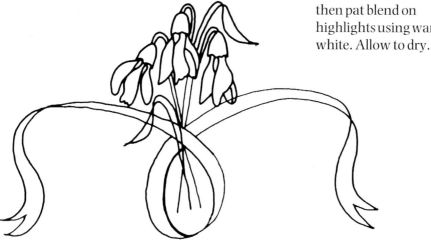

Full-size snowdrop and ribbon pattern

Tulip and snowdrop chest of drawers

I have added a further design to the front of this miniature chest of drawers. The pattern for this can be found opposite. The ribbon is painted in the same way as described on page 86, using a basecoat of dark pink, with light pink highlights. Raw umber is shaded around the outside of the ribbon. You can follow stages 5–8 to paint the snowdrops.

Clematis

The increased spread of trade around the world in the nineteenth century saw plant collectors returning to Britain with many new exotic species. In the middle of that century, two large-flowered clematis were introduced, and that was the beginning of all the lovely hybrids we have today. Clematis come in a variety of stunning colours and sizes; some species have small flowers, while others have blooms as large as 20cm (8in) across.

For this project, I have designed a pattern that is suitable for use on a clock. However, this can easily be adapted to fit on an item of your choice.

This clematis design has been painted using the pat-blending technique shown on pages 96–97. The side-loading technique shown on page 72 has been used in the painting of the flower centres.

A filbert brush is used for this project unless otherwise stated.

You will need

- clock front and mechanism
- acrylic paints: dioxide purple; warm white;
  Turner's yellow; yellow light; Indian red oxide;
  moss green; Payne's grey; transparent magenta;
  carbon black; burgundy
- extender
- No. 8 flat brush
- No. 1 round brush
- liner brush
- stipple brush
- mop brush
- basecoating brush
- transfer paper
- tracing paper
- stylus
- masking tape
- soft pencil or
  felt-tip pen
- chalk or
  watercolour
  crayon
- retarder
- natural sponges:
  1 coarse, 1 fine
- palette knife
- ink nib
- compass

Pattern for the clematis clock
Enlarge on a photocopier by 200%

- **DARK BURGUNDY**
  burgundy + a touch of carbon black
- **MEDIUM PURPLE**
  dioxide purple + a touch of warm white
- **LIGHT YELLOW**
  Turner's yellow + warm white (1:1)
- **LIGHT GREEN**
  yellow light + a touch of carbon black
- **MEDIUM GREEN**
  light green + a touch of carbon black
- **DARK GREEN**
  medium green + a touch of carbon black

Creating the background

Prepare the background in the same way and using the same colours as shown in the realistic marbling demonstration on page 70. Leave to dry before transferring the design (see page 79).

Painting the design

Stage 1

Clematis: Use a No. 8 flat brush to apply a basecoat of medium purple to the flowers. Leave to dry, then transfer the internal petal lines on to the painted surface.

Leaves: Apply a basecoat of light green to the leaves using a No. 8 flat brush.

Stage 2

Clematis: Paint retarder over the flowers. Pat-blend dioxide purple along the edges of each petal, fading out towards the petal centres.

Leaves: Apply retarder to the leaves. Pat-blend dark green at the base of each leaf, fading out towards the tips.

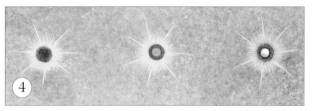

Stage 4

Clematis: Stipple a circle in the centre of each starburst in Indian red oxide. Stipple a smaller circle inside that one in moss green. Stipple a highlight on one side of the green circle in warm white. Use the side-loading technique and a No. 8 flat brush to shade around the outside edge of each circle in Payne's grey.

Stage 3

Clematis: Pat-blend transparent magenta up the centre of each petal. Allow to dry. Use a liner brush and transparent magenta to paint three lines up the centre of each petal. Paint a starburst in the centre of each flower using the tip of a liner brush and light yellow. Work from the centre outwards and build up the strokes gradually by going over and over the same area. Extend the lines slightly up each petal.

Leaves: Pat-blend yellow light at the tip of each leaf, fading out towards the middle. Use a liner brush to paint each stalk in Indian red oxide, and bring the colour up on to the base of each leaf. Pat-blend where the Indian red oxide meets green to blend the colours. Allow to dry.

Stage 5

Clematis: Paint a few highlights on the edges of the petals using a side-loaded No. 8 flat brush and warm white. Where two flowers overlap, make the petals that are on top lighter, and those that are underneath darker.

Leaves: Paint the veins with a liner brush using medium green. Add tendrils to the stalks using a liner brush and Indian red oxide.

Stage 6

Clock face: Transfer the design on to the painted surface. Use an ink nib and dioxide purple to draw on the clock face, and use a liner brush for the line work around the outside. To paint the numbers, fully load a No. 1 round brush with dioxide purple. Press the brush down on the surface to splay the hairs. As you move the brush towards you, lift it very gradually and allow the hairs to come back into a point to create the thin end of the stroke: this is known as the comma stroke.

Assemble the clock hands and mechanism following the manufacturer's instructions.

Clock face pattern
Enlarge on a photocopier by 170%.

⑥

Note

An ink nib is useful for drawing circles or straight lines.

Loading the ink nib	*Drawing a circle*	*Drawing a straight line*
		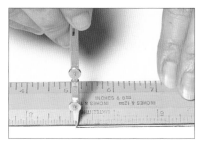
Thin your paint with a little extender until it is the consistency of single cream. Load the tip of a palette knife with paint, then hold it against the reservoir of the pen so that it drips down into the nib.	*Fit the ink nib on to a compass. Extend the compass to create the desired circumference. Move the nib carefully to form a circle, leaning into the curve as you work.*	*Hold a ruler in place on your drawing surface, then run the ink nib along the edge of the ruler, holding the pen upright.*

The finished clematis clock

Decorative
Stamping
for the home

MICHELLE POWELL

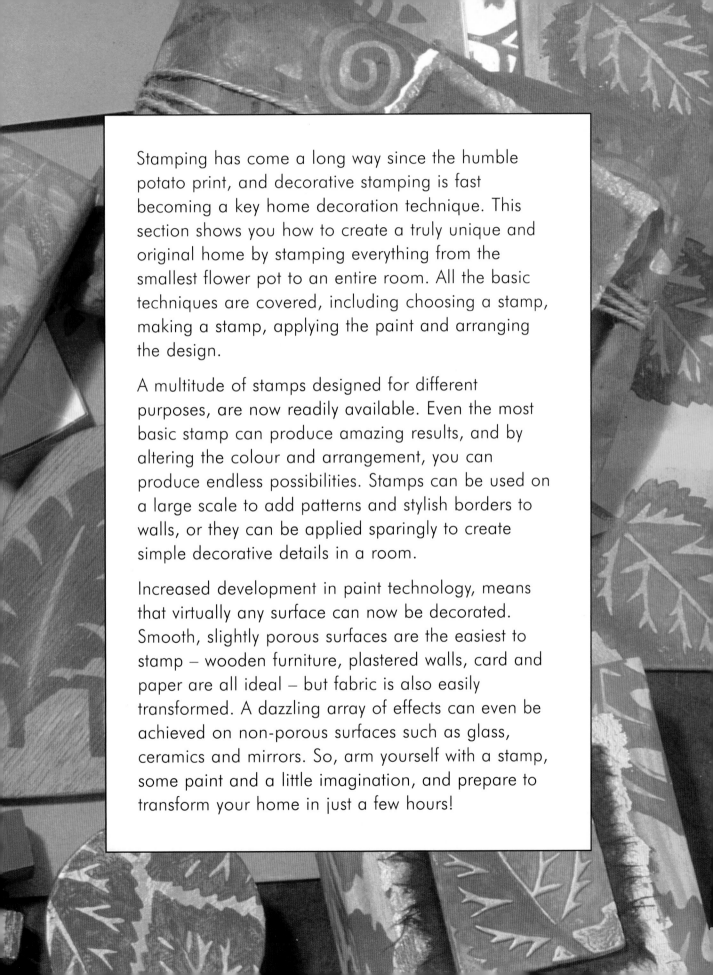

Stamping has come a long way since the humble potato print, and decorative stamping is fast becoming a key home decoration technique. This section shows you how to create a truly unique and original home by stamping everything from the smallest flower pot to an entire room. All the basic techniques are covered, including choosing a stamp, making a stamp, applying the paint and arranging the design.

A multitude of stamps designed for different purposes, are now readily available. Even the most basic stamp can produce amazing results, and by altering the colour and arrangement, you can produce endless possibilities. Stamps can be used on a large scale to add patterns and stylish borders to walls, or they can be applied sparingly to create simple decorative details in a room.

Increased development in paint technology, means that virtually any surface can now be decorated. Smooth, slightly porous surfaces are the easiest to stamp – wooden furniture, plastered walls, card and paper are all ideal – but fabric is also easily transformed. A dazzling array of effects can even be achieved on non-porous surfaces such as glass, ceramics and mirrors. So, arm yourself with a stamp, some paint and a little imagination, and prepare to transform your home in just a few hours!

Materials

In order to create a basic stamped impression, the only materials needed are a stamp, some paint and an applicator sponge. Many paints can be used with decorative stamps, each giving a different effect. Throughout this book, unless otherwise stated, I have used a multipurpose decorative stamping paint that is suitable for stamping any surface, including fabric. It is water-soluble, permanent, acrylic-based and fully opaque.

Stamps

Traditional pictorial rubber stamps have been popular for many years, and these are used for crafting greetings cards and stationery; they are available in many different designs, from elegant images to cute cartoon characters.

Recently, new ranges of stamps designed for a multitude of purposes, have come on the market. Different results can be achieved with each type. Large stamps, with foam, polystyrene or flock surfaces are aimed specifically at creating home decor effects. As foam is slightly porous, it will hold plenty of paint, giving a clear and true stamped impression, especially on wood, walls and fabrics.

The key to choosing a good stamp for decorative stamping is to select one the correct size. If you are embarking on a home decoration project and you have a relatively large area to cover, your stamped image will need to be at least 4cm (1½in) square, preferably even larger (although this will vary depending on purpose and taste). A stamp without fussy detail may render a more pleasing finish.

Try holding the stamp in your hand to check for fit and ease of control. A stamp mounted on a soft foam backing is more forgiving than one with a wooden handle. The foam will bend around curved surfaces and can be pressed into uneven walls.

Other materials

The materials listed here and on pages 116–117 are required for the various techniques in this book. Most are everyday items that you probably already have. More specialist items are available from craft, home decor and DIY stores.

1. **Paintbrushes** I use a selection, including large decorator's brushes for backgrounds, and small paintbrushes for detailing.

2. **Wedge applicator sponges** Used to apply paint to and blend colours on a stamp.

3. **Plate** This is used as a palette.

4. **Various decorative stamping paints** Used for stamping, and for adding detail.

5. **Emulsion paint** This is used for basecoating, or painting walls and small furniture.

6. **Wallpaper paste** This can be mixed with paint to make it more translucent and to increase the open drying time, which is useful when stamping off. Glycerine can be used instead.

7. **Glycerine** This can be mixed with paint to add translucency, and increase open drying time.

8. **Air-hardening clay** You can press a stamp into soft clay to create an embossed pattern.

9. **Craft knife** For cutting clay.

10. **Nailbrush** For cleaning stamps.

11. **Damp cloth** Useful in case of mistakes, and for wiping up spillages.

12. **Soft cloth** For applying and buffing up wax.

13. **Scrap paper** You can create large masks from this. A pile of scrap paper should also be placed under thin fabric when stamping.

14. **Sticky notelets** These can be used to create small masks.

15. **Ruler** Used for measuring and cutting against.

16. **Cutting mat** For working on when using a scalpel.

17. **Dutch metal leaf** Used to gild.

18. **Gilding size** For attaching Dutch metal leaf.

19. **Soft brush** For brushing off excess metal leaf.

20. **Cotton buds** For applying dots of paint.

21. **Tailor's chalk** For marking fabric.

22. **Scalpel** For cutting out paper masks, foam for a stamp, and for other precision cutting.

23. **Pencil** For general use, including marking out a design.

24. **Tracing paper** Used to trace an image when making a stamp.

25. **MDF block** Medium-density fibreboard is used as a backing for a homemade stamp.

26. **High-density foam** Used to make a stamp.

27. **Wood dowel** A square of foam can be glued to the end of dowelling to make a small stamp.

28. **Glitter and glue pen** Used to add decoration to stamped images.

29. **Glue** An adhesive stick is used to adhere tracing paper to foam when making a stamp. Solvent glue is for general use.

30. **Iron** For fixing stamped fabric.

31. **Masking tape** Both normal and low-tack tape are used (depending on the surface) for masking off areas from paint.

32. **Water sprayer** For dampening a stamp when working on velvet (see page 144).

33. **Furniture wax** Used to protect a wooden stamped piece. If tinted, it can be used to colour.

34. **Gilding wax (gold and copper)** This can be rubbed in to create a subtle metallic effect.

35. **Tile varnish** This protects the painted or stamped images by sealing the surface.

36. **Water-based varnish** Used for varnish stamping, frosted stamping and for sealing.

Making a stamp

You can custom-make stamps from a number of different materials. I find the best results are achieved using high-density foam, as detailed images can be easily cut out. I have used a piece of MDF (medium density fibreboard) for the stamp handle, but any wood will do as long as it is thick enough to hold comfortably.

Inspiration for stamp designs can come from many sources – wallpaper, fabric and greetings cards, for example, or you can use your own artwork. In this demonstration I have taken a flower motif from curtain fabric.

1. Place a piece of tracing paper over your chosen design and go around the outline with a pencil.

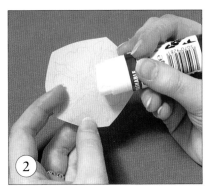

2. Cut very roughly around the outside of the design. Use an adhesive stick to add a little glue to the back of the tracing paper then press it on to a piece of thin high-density foam.

3. Place the foam and design on a cutting mat, and cut around the shapes of the design using a scalpel. Work slowly and carefully and try to keep the blade as upright as possible as you work.

4. Arrange the foam pieces on a small block of MDF or wood. Use solvent glue to stick the foam pieces down.

OPPOSITE
This coordinating lampshade and border are stamped with homemade stamps inspired by curtain fabric. Two stamps are cut out – a flower and a leaf – and they are alternated to create a simple but effective design.

Basic techniques

There are many methods of creating an image with a stamp. For most decorative effects, paint is used rather than an ink pad. The paint can be applied in a number of ways, including with a paintbrush, a wedge applicator sponge or a sponge roller. A wedge applicator sponge is the most versatile tool for applying paint. It is quick and easy to use and gives an even covering of paint to the correct thickness. This method also allows any number of colours to be applied to one stamp to create stunning multicoloured impressions and soft, subtle colour blending.

Note

If you make a mistake, wipe away the stamped image using a clean damp cloth. Wash the stamp, reapply the paint and start again!

You can touch up an image using a small paintbrush.

1. Decant pools of paint on to a palette. Press a wedge applicator sponge into your first colour.

2. Press the paint into the sponge using the side of the palette, then dab the sponge on to the stamp.

3. Apply a second colour using a clean applicator sponge. Turn the sponge round and use a clean corner to blot over the line and blend the colours together.

4. Apply additional colours. Press the stamp firmly on to your surface. Press each area of the stamp down evenly.

5. Hold your surface still and then lift the stamp straight up, without tilting it or shifting its position.

6. Place the stamp in a basin of water or under a tap. Scrub gently with a soft nailbrush to clean the stamp. Leave to dry.

Different results can be achieved with a single stamp by simply varying the colour combination.

Creative stamping

Varied and exciting effects are easy to achieve using varnishes, glazes and gilding size rather than paint for stamping. Try experimenting with other materials to create techniques of your own.

Stamping with varnish

This technique uses varnish to act as a resist. The following demonstration is worked using a clear, water-based satin varnish, but you could use any clear varnish. This technique works best on smooth surfaces, particularly wood.

1. Apply clear varnish to the stamp using an applicator sponge, then press onto your surface. Leave until fully dry.

2. Mix one part paint to one part water to create a colour-wash. Dab a clean cloth into the paint mixture and then wipe over the surface and over the varnished image. Leave to dry.

__Playing card box__
A subtle effect can be created using a simple varnish-stamped motif. A wash of paint is applied to highlight the image and bring out the natural grain of the wood.

Stamping off

This technique uses the stamp to remove paint, and it is achieved with two colours. You can use dark on light or light on dark. You get a subtler effect if you use two shades of the same colour, as shown here. The stamping off technique is only effective if you work quickly as the topcoat can only be stamped off while it is still wet.

Note
When stamping off, mix wallpaper paste or glycerine into the paint to give it a longer open drying time.

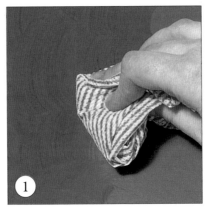

1. Apply a basecoat of paint then leave to dry. Mix up a second colour mixture using one part paint to three parts ready-mixed wallpaper paste. Dip a cloth into this mixture and then wipe over the basecoat in random swirling strokes.

2. Press a clean dry stamp on to the painted surface and then remove it. If you are stamping off lots of images, repeat, working quickly so as not to allow the topcoat to dry.

Place mat
Create a stylish place mat by stamping off a darker top coat of paint to reveal a lighter base coat colour.

Frosted stamping

This is a very effective decorative technique which uses varnish mixed with white paint, to produce a frosted glass effect. It is a good idea to apply a coat of clear acrylic varnish to protect your finished piece.

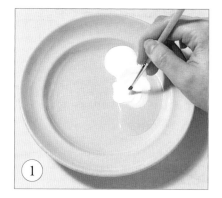

1. Decant one part clear water-based varnish and one part white paint on to a clean palette. Mix together thoroughly.

2. Apply the paint mixture to the stamp, and then press the stamp lightly on to a glass surface, taking great care not to let the stamp slide. Leave to dry.

Glass vase
Transform a plain vase quickly and simply by using a translucent mix of paint and varnish to stamp a frosted image.

Gilding

You can apply gilding size to a stamp and use it to create brilliant metallic gilded images. The size acts like glue, so when the Dutch metal leaf is applied, it adheres only to the stamped image.

1. Apply size to a stamp and then stamp on to your surface. Leave to dry for approximately five minutes, until the size goes clear but still feels tacky.

2. Place a sheet of Dutch metal leaf over the stamped size. Press the leaf on to the size by tapping it lightly with a soft, clean, dry paintbrush. Use the same brush to brush off the leaf and reveal the gilded image.

Candlestick
Add elegance to your stamping by creating gilded images using size and Dutch metal leaf.

Note
Clean the stamp immediately after use with warm water and a soft nailbrush. Never allow size to dry on a stamp.

Arranging a design

Stamping is a fascinating technique, with huge potential. Initially, it may be difficult to see how a single stamped image can be used to create a whole interior scheme. However, just by altering the colour used on a stamp you can create a different look. With multiple stamped images, endless permutations of design and layout are possible. Stamp images in rows to create stripes, up and down for zig-zags, randomly all over, or in small clusters. Once started, you will soon find that more and more ideas will flow.

Certain images lend themselves better to certain designs. Look at the outer shape of the stamp. One that is basically square or rectangular will be best suited for rigid stripe or border designs. A stamp with a very irregular outline can create interesting random or cluster patterns.

Some stamps have a definite right way up – bear this in mind when stamping, but remember that you can still deploy a certain amount of artistic license. There are no rules in stamping; if you think an image looks effective stamped upside down, then stamp it that way!

If you are unsure of your chosen design, stamp several images on scrap paper before you begin your project. Cut out the images roughly, then move them around until you are happy with the design.

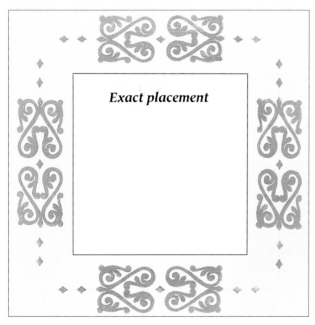

Some projects require exact placement of stamped images. For this design, the image is stamped several times on to acetate and a cross is drawn in the centre of each image. A cross is then drawn on the back of the stamp, in exactly the same place. The acetate images are moved around on the surface to find the best positioning for the design. The crosses are transferred from the acetate sheet to the stamping surface. The crosses on the surface are then lined up with the cross on the stamp for perfect positioning.

This design is worked by ruling two lines on the surface, with the gap in between, the approximate size of the stamp. The stamps are then applied between these lines and are spaced by eye. If working on a small object, start by stamping one image in the centre then fill in either side. Try alternating two or three different images or creating multiple rows of stamped images. If exact positioning is required, cut a strip of card the width of the desired gap and use this as a spacer between the stamps.

Clustered design

Random design

This design is stamped by varying the position of the image and then over-stamping with a second image. A cluster of stamped images is ideal for decorating small irregular-shaped spaces. Try to avoid filling all the available space.

This design is stamped randomly, varying the position of each stamp. Spacing is important: on smaller projects, the stamped images need to be quite close together; if stamping a large wall, the images can afford to be spaced 0.5–1m (2–3ft) apart.

Structured all-over design

Naturalistic arrangement

Checks, diamonds, stripes and zig-zags are all structured patterns, where exact positioning is needed. Pencil lines are ruled to indicate the central position of the stamped image on the surface. The centre top and centre bottom are marked on the back of the stamp, and the dots are then matched up with the pencil lines.

This trompe l'oeil effect is created by positioning the stamped images by eye, in natural-looking clusters. The images in the foreground are masked and further images are then stamped in the background several times without reapplying paint, so that they begin to get more faint.

WOOD, PLASTER, PAPER AND CARD

Gilded writing slope • Floral hat box • Gothic mirror Children's toy box

Paper is the obvious material to start stamping on. It is cheap, easy to use and readily available. For any project, I would recommend practising first on scrap paper to get used to the feel of the stamp and to experiment with colour combinations. Any paper or card that has a smooth surface is excellent for stamping on, and no special technique is needed. Textured paper or card can also be used, but you should stamp carefully to ensure the image is crisp. There are many beautiful handmade papers available and these can be stamped to create luxurious writing paper, gift wrap and greetings cards. Paper is also the ideal medium to cover other items with, as you can stamp on the paper whilst it is flat, and then glue it to a three-dimensional object – a notebook, storage box or small piece of furniture, for example.

Wood is also an ideal stamping surface. You can stamp on to any real wood whether it is untreated, varnished, waxed or painted. Ensure the wood is clean and free from dust before you begin. If you are stamping on to untreated wood, sand it to a reasonably smooth finish first. Take care when stamping wooden surfaces covered with gloss paint or varnish, as the stamp may slide. Protect a finished wooden piece by applying a couple of coats of any clear matt, satin or gloss varnish.

Stamping is also perfect for plastered walls, particularly those painted with emulsion. Before stamping, clean the walls with a damp cloth to ensure that they are grease- and dust-free. If you are stamping on to newly-painted walls, make sure you wait until they are fully dry. As you are stamping on to a vertical rather than a horizontal surface, you must remember to press evenly all over the back of the stamp to ensure a clear image. When stamping a whole room, start at the top and work down the wall so that you do not smudge the images you have just stamped.

Gilded writing slope

The changing shapes and colours of autumnal leaves inspired the design for this pine writing slope. The slope is first stained using instant coffee to give a very rich, natural look, and it is finished with clear wax which produces a subtle, warm sheen. Three gilded leaf images add a sophisticated touch, making this writing slope ideal for the home, office or study.

You will need
Writing slope
Medium grade sandpaper
Damp cloth
Boiling water
Instant coffee
Cup and teaspoon
6.5cm (2½in) paintbrush
Small paintbrush
Decorative stamping paint: green, terracotta, brown, red, yellow and black
Decorative stamps: two different leaves
Gold Dutch metal leaf
Gilding size
Clean, soft, dry brush
Clear furniture wax
Clean, soft cloth
Glycerine
Applicator sponges and palette
Low-tack masking tape
Pencil and ruler

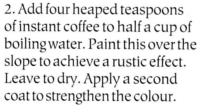

1. Prepare the wooden surface by lightly sanding all over using medium grade sandpaper. Wipe with a damp cloth to remove all traces of dust.

2. Add four heaped teaspoons of instant coffee to half a cup of boiling water. Paint this over the slope to achieve a rustic effect. Leave to dry. Apply a second coat to strengthen the colour.

3. Transfer pools of green, terracotta, brown, red, yellow and black paint on to a palette. For each colour, mix approximately one part paint to one part glycerine – this will give a translucent finish to the paints.

4. Apply green, brown and yellow to one of the leaf stamps using an applicator sponge. Blend the colours on the stamp (see page 120). Stamp a random pattern over the desk lid. Repeat with the second leaf stamp to fill in the spaces, using terracotta, red, brown, black and yellow. Leave to dry.

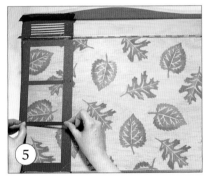

5. Mark three 9cm (3½in) squares down the left-hand side of the lid, 2cm (¾in) from the edge. On the top, mark five thin stripes, approximately 9 x 0.5cm (3½ x ¼in). Use lengths of low-tack masking tape to mask the surrounding area and between the stripes.

6. Load a 6.5cm (2½in) brush with black, brown and red paint and use this to stipple over the squares on the lid, and the stripes on the top (see step 4, page 169). Leave to dry. Remove the masking tape.

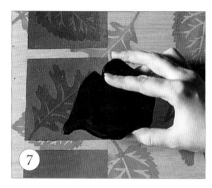

7. Apply gilding size to the stamp using a sponge applicator (see page 125) and stamp centrally on to the brown squares. Leave the size to dry for about five minutes, until it goes clear, but is just tacky.

8. Lay gold metal leaf over the size and tap down with a clean, soft, dry brush (see page 125). Brush away any excess gold leaf. Use these scraps to fill in any small gaps. Leave to dry overnight.

Note
If you rub the bristles of a clean, dry paintbrush over your hair, you will create static. You can use this static to pick up scraps of gold leaf.

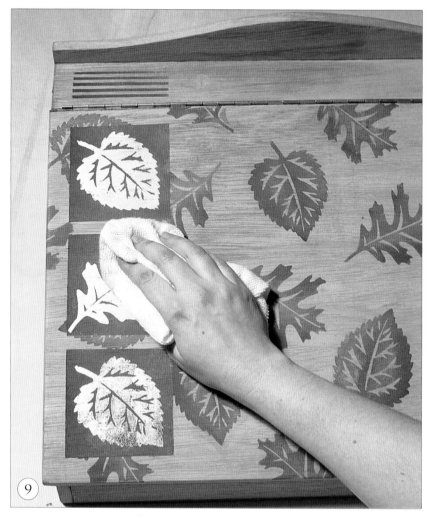

9. Rub over the entire writing slope using clear furniture wax and a soft cloth. This will seal the colours and create a hardwearing finish.

OPPOSITE
Gilded writing slope
This writing slope features gilded leaf motifs and blended multicoloured stamping. It is easy to create a great variety of matching writing paper and desk accessories. Here I have stamped the leaf on to small squares of paper, combined these with roughly gilded squares and squares of handmade paper and then glued them into position on an ink bottle and note book. The fabric on the noticeboard is also decorated using the leaf stamps.

Floral hat box

This pretty floral stamped box creates stylish storage and is perfect for organising treasured possessions. The box I have used is approximately 15cm (6in) tall, with a diameter of 27cm (10½in). If your box is a different size, then you will need to adjust the length of muslin needed; this should be approximately three-and-a-half times the diameter of the box. The hat box I have used has eyelet holes for threading the cord handle. If your box does not have holes, these can be easily made using a bradawl or eyelet pliers. Alternatively, you can omit the handle.

You will need

Hat box, 27cm (10½in) in diameter, 15cm (6in) high

Emulsion paint: lilac

2.5cm (1in) paintbrush

Small paintbrush

Decorative stamping paint: purple, lavender, mid-green, jade, dusty pink, pale pink and white

Decorative stamps: daisy, anemone, leaves

Applicator sponges and palette

Cotton buds

Pencil and ruler

Purple muslin, 15 x 80cm (6 x 31½in)

Thin purple cord, 65cm (26in)

Scrap paper

Sticky notelets

Solvent glue

Scalpel and cutting mat

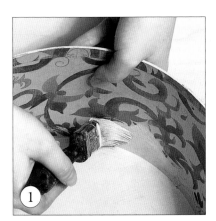

1. Apply a coat of lilac emulsion to the inside and outside of the hat box, and the inside and outside of the lid. Leave to dry before applying another coat. Leave to dry.

2. Blend purple and lavender on the daisy stamp (see page 120). Stamp at equal intervals around the box, leaving enough space in between each image for the anemone stamp. Leave to dry.

3. Blend pale pink, dusty pink and lavender on the anemone stamp and then use this to stamp in between the daisies. Leave to dry.

4. Stamp the daisy on to a sticky notelet. Leave to dry before cutting around the outline of the shape using a scalpel; this will create a mask. Repeat with the anemone stamp.

Note
You may find it easier to make several masks of each flower for this project. To do this, peel off a few sticky notelets together, stamp on to the top one and then cut through all the layers at once.

If you want to make reusable masks, stamp the images on to acetate then cut them out. Use a re-positionable spray adhesive to lightly coat the back of the masks each time you want to use them. Clean with water after use.

5. Position the masks directly over the stamped images. Blend mid-green and jade on the leaf stamp and then stamp between the flowers. Repeat all around the box, then remove the masks and leave to dry.

6. Dip the end of a cotton bud into white paint and use this to create small clusters of dots at the edges of the flowers to represent gypsophila.

7. Divide the lid into an equal number of sections. To do this, wrap a long strip of scrap paper around the circumference of the lid. Trim the ends where they meet. Fold the strip in half, then in half again and continue folding until the paper is the width you would like the stripe on the lid. Unfold the paper and wrap it around the box. Use a pencil to mark the lid at each paper fold.

(8)

(9)

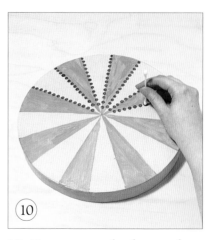

(10)

8. Join up the pencil marks on the lid to make stripes. Try to leave only very faint pencil lines.

9. Mix a little purple decorative stamping paint with lavender. Use a small paintbrush to paint every other stripe. Do not worry if the edges of the stripes are not very neat. Leave to dry.

10. Use a cotton bud to apply an evenly spaced row of purple dots along the edges of the stripes. Leave to dry.

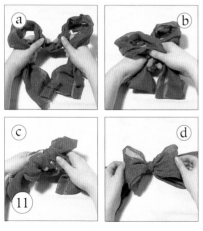

(a) (b)
(c) (d)
(11)

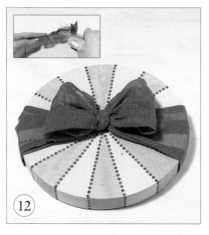

(12)

(13)

11. Form two loops in the centre of the length of purple muslin (a). Cross one of the loops over the other (b) and then bring the crossed-over loop up through the hole (c). Arrange the fabric to form a bow (d).

12. Use solvent glue to attach each end of the muslin fabric inside the rim of the lid.

13. Thread purple cord through the holes in the side of the hat box to make a handle. Knot the cord on the inside to secure it.

OPPOSITE
Floral hat boxes
These stamped flowers are masked and then the background between is filled in with leaves. When the masks are removed, the leaves appear to be behind the flowers. Floral stamps lend themselves particularly well to being grouped to make long swags or wreaths, as shown by the fire screen. You can alter the shades of the flowers to match an existing colour scheme, or use the technique to add small decorative details to existing furniture.

Gothic mirror

For this project, I have used a very unusual mirror. Look for something similar in junk shops, or approach a local carpenter to make one specially for you. Whatever mirror you choose to decorate, you can adapt this technique to suit.

Before you start, you will need to hand cut the key and Tudor stamps using the patterns provided. Trace off the images and follow the instructions given on page 118. Alternatively, you could use a pre-cut stamp of your choice.

You will need
Mirror frame
MDF block
High-density foam
Scalpel
Cutting mat
Tracing paper
Pencil
Adhesive stick
Solvent glue
Emulsion paint: yellow and
  dark yellow
Decorative stamping paint:
  mid-green, dark green,
  brown, red and dark yellow
Applicator sponges and palette
Wallpaper paste
Sand or sawdust
Powdered filler
5cm (2in) paintbrush
1cm (½in) paintbrush
Clear acrylic matt varnish

Full-size patterns for the Tudor and Key stamps

1. Remove the mirror glass and doors. Lightly sand if necessary. Mix one part sand (or sawdust) with one part yellow emulsion and one part powdered filler. Add one part water if the mixture is too dry.

2. Stipple a coat of this mixture on to the mirror frame and doors. Leave to dry.

3. Mix a wash using three parts wallpaper paste to one part dark yellow emulsion paint and apply this to the frame. Press the clean key stamp onto the wet paint using the stamping off technique to create a subtle pattern (see page 123).

4. Apply dark green, mid-green, dark yellow, red, dark pink and brown paint to the Tudor stamp. Stamp the image on the inside of one of the door panels, so that the bottom of the stamp roughly lines up with the centre. Load the stamp with paint again, turn it upside down then line it up with the bottom of the first stamp. Repeat on the other door.

5. Mix one part red paint with one part dark pink paint, one part sand (or sawdust) and one part powdered filler. Stipple this mixture over the wooden decorative trim, the coving and the moulding on the frame using a 1cm (½in) brush. Reattach the mirror glass and doors to the frame. Finish with a coat of clear acrylic matt varnish, applied in a stippling action to add to the aged, rustic look.

Gothic mirror

Reminiscent of times gone by, this Gothic styled mirror makes a stunning centrepiece for any room and the plant pot complements it perfectly. Two different stamping techniques are used, stamping off and stamping on, to give a rich layered effect. The key and Tudor stamps used are hand-cut from thin, high-density foam.

Children's toy box

You can decorate a toy chest with a patchwork of pastel shapes and patterns. Pearlescent paint is used throughout this project to create a soft shimmer to the stamping. The pearlescent paint is made by mixing equal parts of coloured paint with silver paint. Glitter is added for extra sparkle, and dimensional outlining paste is used to create the effect of stitching between the different stamped patches. Masking tape is used to section off each area, making it easy to combine many different colours and patterns on one box. The same technique can be used to create a matching lid.

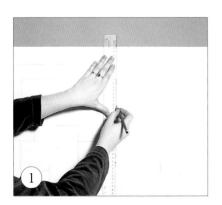

1. Paint the chest with white emulsion paint. Leave to dry then apply a second coat. Leave to dry. Use a pencil and ruler to mark random patchwork squares all over the box. The sizes and shapes do not matter, as long as they are large enough to allow room for the stamped images.

2. Mask some of the areas off with masking tape. Mix one part lavender paint with one part silver paint and two parts ready-mixed wallpaper paste. Use a rag to move this paint mixture around within the masked shapes to create an uneven finish. Leave to dry.

3. Mix one part lavender paint to one part silver paint to give a pearlescent effect. Stamp swirls within some of the lilac shapes, and leave others unstamped.

4. Remove the masking tape and repeat steps 2 and 3 with other colours and the leaf and flower stamps. Change stamps and colours randomly. Leave to dry. Continue until the box is covered.

5. Stamp bugs on to some of the squares, using colours of your choice. Blend the colours on the stamp before stamping (see page 120). Leave to dry.

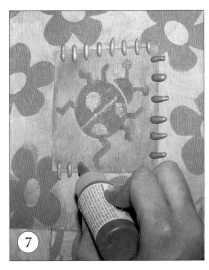

6. Apply glue to the spots on the bugs' wings, the antennae, and the central wing lines. Sprinkle with glitter then leave to dry.

7. Use dimensional outlining paste to draw small lines and crosses around the edges of the shapes; this will represent patchwork stitching. Leave to dry. Apply a coat of clear matt acrylic varnish.

Children's toy box
Pearlescent pastel colours give this toy box a whimsical quality, making it ideal for a young child's room. The patchwork effect is created by masking separate areas, stamping, then adding stitch detailing with outlining paste. Small pictures are stamped to match.

FABRICS

Eastern clothes screen • Ethnic throw

Decorative stamping is an ideal way to decorate plain fabric, perhaps to match with an existing scheme or to jazz up older furnishings. Most fabrics can be stamped successfully, but cotton or cotton-mix fabrics with a fine, close weave are ideal. Using the correct paint is crucial if you want your stamped images to be washable. Multi-purpose stamping paints suitable for use on fabrics are available, as well as paints designed specifically for use on fabric. Follow the manufacturer's instructions carefully for best results.

Wash, dry and iron all fabrics before stamping, to remove any dirt and the manufacturer's dressing. Paint will seep through fabric when you are stamping, so it is best to work on a flat surface, protected with scrap paper or several layers of old sheeting. Heavy or thick fabrics may need an extra thick layer of paint in order to achieve even coverage. If this is the case, apply the paint to the stamp using a paintbrush, rather than an applicator sponge. Try not to move the fabric while you are stamping, as the wet paint that seeps on to the backing paper or sheeting may mark the underside of the fabric. When the paint is dry, you should iron on the reverse side of the fabric to fix the paint; set the iron at a temperature suitable for the fabric you are working on.

The only fabrics that are difficult to stamp are those with a very large weave or slub. Some 100% synthetic fabrics will not take the paint very well. For practicality, any fabric that you cannot iron is unsuitable as you are unable to fix the paints. To clean stamped items, use a cool wash, or hand wash them. All home-use fabric paints will start to fade after repeated washing.

Note

It is possible to stamp on velvet, without using paint! Spray the clean stamp with a water sprayer. Place the velvet on top of the stamp, plush side down, facing the front of the image. Press the velvet above the stamp using an iron on a medium setting. Hold the iron in place for two seconds, then lift up for a moment before  pressing it down again for one second. The pile of the velvet will depress in the shape of the stamp to leave a subtle image, that will catch the light.

Eastern clothes screen

Replace old or worn-out fabric on a screen with delicate stamped muslin panels. I have worked three panels – two in rust and one in cream, but you could work other combinations. When stamping on fabric such as muslin, remember to protect your work surface with layers of paper or old sheeting, as the paint will go straight through.

I have not given specific fabric sizes for this project as all screens will vary. Before you begin, remove any fabric from the existing screen, and use this as a template for cutting the new fabric panels; remember to leave a 2cm (¾in) seam allowance on all sides. Wash, dry and iron the new fabric.

You will need

Iron or wooden screen frame

Cream muslin: two 15cm (6in) squares, one 8cm (3¼in) square, one panel piece

Rust muslin: one 15cm (6in) square, two 8cm (3¼in) squares, two panel pieces

Gold organza: three 11cm (4¼in) squares

4m (4yd) rust ribbon and 2m (2yd) cream ribbon

Scrap paper or old sheeting

Rust and cream sewing thread

Decorative stamping paint: rust, gold and cream

Decorative stamp: wrought iron shape

Applicator sponges and palette

Pins

Scissors

Iron

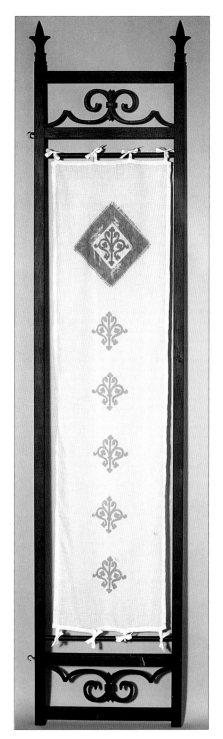

1. Lay one of the muslin panel pieces out on a smooth flat surface, on top of a layer of paper or old sheeting. Apply gold paint to your stamp then stamp a row of images down the centre of the panel, beginning approximately 38cm (15in) from the top. Try to hold the fabric flat as you stamp.

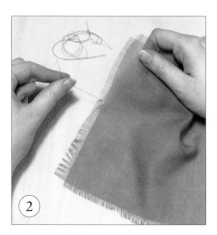

2. Remove threads from the edges of each fabric square to create a 3mm (1/8in) frayed edge.

3. Apply rust paint to the stamp then stamp one image in each of the four corners of the large rust squares. Now stamp cream images on the large cream fabric squares.

5. Arrange the squares on top of each other with the smallest on top, and the gold organza in the middle.

4. Apply rust paint to the stamp then stamp one image in the centre of each of the small cream squares. Now stamp cream images on the small rust fabric squares. Leave the gold organza un-stamped.

(6)

6. Position the squares centrally at the top of the muslin panels then pin them in place. Sew a line of zig-zag stitch around the largest square, and around the smallest square. Try to sew approximately 0.5cm (¼in) in from the edge.

7. Turn the fabric in twice to form a 1cm (⅜in) hem, and machine stitch all round. Iron the fabric to fix the paint. Cut eight 25cm (9in) lengths of ribbon for each panel. Fold the ribbon in half and hand sew to the top edge of the fabric panel. Use four pieces at the top and four pieces at the bottom of each panel. Tie the fabric to the screen.

(7)

Ethnic throw

The beauty of this project lies in the random selection of stamped fabrics, colours and patterns. You can use up any oddments of plain fabrics you have to create a lively ethnic patchwork. If recycling fabrics, remember to wash, dry and iron them all before you start. Smooth, close-weave fabrics give the best results when stamping.

Note
Lay the heavy mustard fabric out before cutting. If it has an attractive selvedge, then do not try to trim or fray this. The selvedge will require no sewing.

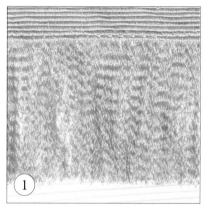

1. Pull out some of the weft threads from the edges of the heavy mustard fabric to create a 5cm (2in) frayed fringe. Sew a line of zig-zag stitch along the line where the fraying stops, to secure the edge.

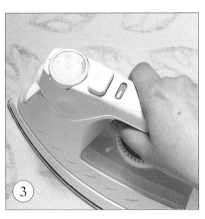

3. Iron the back of each piece of stamped fabric to fix the design. Adjust the setting on the iron to one that is suitable for the fabric you are ironing.

2. Stamp the cream, purple, yellow, beige and orange fabrics randomly all over using one or a selection of stamps and a colour of your choice. I have used paints to tone with the fabrics. As the fabric is quite thick, apply the paint with a small paintbrush rather than with an applicator sponge. Leave the paint to dry for at least twenty-four hours.

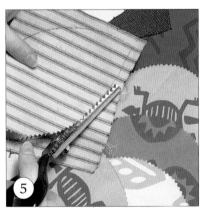

5. Cut leaf shapes out of some of the squares using pinking shears. Cut others down into smaller squares using the straight-edge scissors. Create a fringe around some of the small squares if you wish (see step 1).

4. Cut each piece of stamped fabric, the ticking and the green open weave fabric into 15cm (6in) squares.

6. Arrange the squares and leaves on top of each other. Try to be completely random and mix different colours and patterns. Sew the shapes together with a zig-zag stitch.

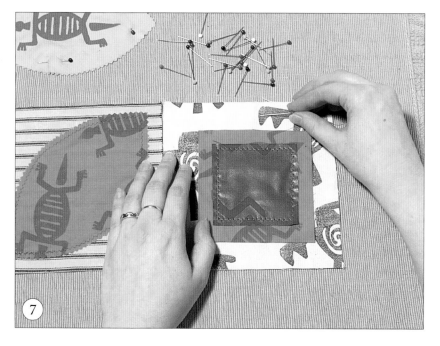

7. Lay the fabric squares on to the mustard backing fabric to create a border around the edge. I arranged some leaves within the border, and positioned four squares in the centre, but you can move the squares and leaves around until you are happy with the overall design. Pin to secure, and then sew in place.

Ethnic throw
This colourful throw is made up of appliquéd patches of stamped fabrics which are assembled to give an African flavour. You can use this technique to style a matching picture and wall hanging.

CERAMICS, GLASS AND METAL

Citrus cupboard • Terracotta pot • Mediterranean table
Primitive picture frame

Very smooth non-porous surfaces can be quite difficult to stamp on as the paint has nothing to adhere to. It is worth spending time experimenting before undertaking any large project on an unusual surface. Three factors can affect the results achieved: the surface itself; the type of paint used; and the application technique.

Unglazed ceramics such as terracotta pots and biscuit-ware china present no real problems regarding paint application. However, glass, mirror, metal and glazed ceramics such as tiles and domestic china, have a completely non-porous surface and the stamping technique needs to vary slightly to allow for this. A stamp fully loaded with paint will tend to slide on the shiny surface. A specialist decorative stamping paint or an acrylic paint should be used and the minimum of paint should be applied to the stamp. To do this, load the stamp with paint, stamp on to a scrap piece of paper then, without reapplying paint, stamp on to your surface. When the paint is dry, apply several coats of tile varnish or clear acrylic car lacquer to seal the stamping.

Alternatively, you can purchase paints designed to work on specific surfaces: thermo-hardening ceramic paints fire in a domestic oven and specialist glass and mirror paints are also available. These paints all work with stamps but tend to give a very soft, pale, translucent colour. There are also primers now available which will prepare virtually any surface for painting or stamping. Always experiment first and follow the manufacturer's instructions with care.

A frosted decorative stamping effect can be worked on glass and mirror (see page 124) or the surfaces can be stamped with neat or diluted paint. Before you begin, the surface should be prepared by washing with soapy water to remove any grease. It should then be allowed to dry thoroughly. Both effects will withstand gentle washing, but are unsuitable for food containers or anything that requires regular washing. Protect the stamped images from chipping by applying several coats of clear acrylic car lacquer when dry.

Most sheet metal is supplied with a protective plastic film covering so no surface preparation is necessary, you simply need to remove the film. If your metal does not have this film, ensure the surface is free from dust and grease before you begin.

Citrus cupboard

Any small wooden cupboard is suitable to restyle for this project, but unfinished pine is ideal. The lemon stamped design and crisp, clean aluminium make this an ideal cupboard for a modern kitchen. Lemon emulsion paint is thinned with water to give a soft woodwash effect, so a small tester pot of paint should be sufficient to cover the piece. Try changing or painting the handles on an older cupboard to bring it up-to-date, or add a length of dowel for hanging utensils. You can alter the colour scheme and stamp to adapt this project for any room – woodwash with lime and stamp fish and shells for the bathroom, or stain the wood dark oak and stamp with classical flourishes for a grand dining room.

You will need

Wooden cupboard
Medium grade sandpaper
Damp cloth
0.5mm (0.020in) aluminium sheet
Large rounded nail
Small pointed nail
Hammer
Silicone glue
Emulsion paint: lemon
Decorative stamping paint: jade, dark green, yellow, orange, white, lemon and silver
Decorative stamps: lemons; lemon slices; and swirls
Sponge applicators and palette
1cm (½in) square piece of foam
Short length of dowel, or old thick marker pen
Solvent glue
Thin plywood (cut to fit the door panels)
Soft cloth
2.5cm (1in) masking tape
Cutting mat
Steel ruler
Scalpel
Old blanket or newspapers
Scrap paper
Sticky notelets
5 chrome-plated handles

1. Prepare the wooden surface in the same way as the writing slope (see step 1, page 130). Dilute the lemon emulsion paint using five parts water to one part paint. Apply a coat all over the cupboard. Leave to dry.

Note

If you are using an old cupboard, remove all paint or varnish using a paint stripper. Follow the manufacturer's instructions carefully. Sand thoroughly to remove any remaining paint. Wear a face mask to avoid inhaling paint or varnish dust.

2. Paint the plywood panels using dark green decorative stamping paint. Leave to dry. Mix a small amount of jade green to the dark green to make a slightly lighter green. Use this colour to stamp swirls all over the plywood panels.

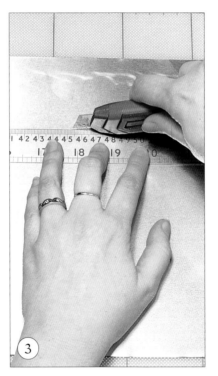

Note
You can use large old scissors to cut out the aluminium if you prefer. This will not, however, produce such a smooth line.

3. Cut two pieces of aluminium, each one to fit inside the door frame, allowing a 5cm (2in) gap all around. To do this, work on a cutting mat and use a steel ruler to get a straight edge. Make a series of small cuts, pressing lightly until you have created a deep groove, then bend the joint back and forth until the metal snaps.

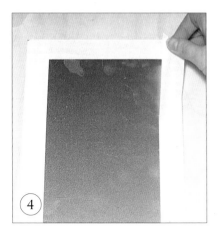

4. Use masking tape to mask all around the edge of both of the aluminium panels.

5. Apply dark green, jade, orange, yellow and lemon paint to your lemon stamp using a sponge applicator. Blend the colours (see page 120) then stamp on to both metal panels. As the aluminium is a very non-absorbent surface, stamp first on to scrap paper, and then on to the metal. Take care not to let the stamp slide on the metal.

6. Mask the lemon (see page 135) on each panel. Apply silver paint to the swirls stamp and stamp all over both central areas. Leave to dry before removing the masking tape and the lemon mask.

7. Glue a 1cm (½in) square of foam on to the end of an old pen lid or a piece of dowel to make a small square stamp. Apply yellow and orange paint then stamp a border around each metal panel. Leave to dry.

8. Place one of the metal panels on a folded old blanket or a pile of newspaper. Use a hammer and a large rounded nail to punch dents into the metal. Hammer lightly to avoid punching straight through the metal. Use this technique to add a central vein to each leaf, and then scratch in smaller veins using the tip of a small pointed nail. Continue adding dents to create a border pattern around the panel. Repeat with the other metal panel.

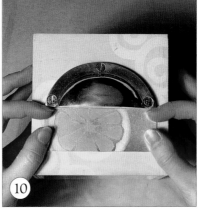

10. Stamp areas of the drawers using pale yellow and the swirls stamp. Leave to dry. Screw the handles in place. Decorate with small pieces of aluminium stamped using the lemon slice stamp. Glue them to the front of the drawers.

9. Use silicone glue to stick each metal panel centrally on to the plywood. Leave to set, then stick the pieces of plywood on to the doors of the cupboard.

Citrus cupboard

The stylish punched aluminium effect is easy to create and adds decorative detail to the stamped design. To finish this cupboard, I cut a piece of thick dowel the inside width of the cupboard, painted it dark green, then attached it to the cupboard using wardrobe rail fittings, to create extra storage. I also rubbed clear furniture wax into the finished piece to protect it. Matching kitchen accessories have been stamped, including a trompe l'oeil effect lemon tree which is made up of many stamped images and includes a hand-painted trunk and pot.

Terracotta pot

Jazz up terracotta pots with decorative stamping, ageing effects and lashings of colour. Choose your stamp carefully: a large stamp is easier to apply to a large pot than a small one. If your pot is very small, then stick to a small stamp or just decorate the rim. Foam-backed stamps are ideal as they will curve around the pot. If decorating an old pot, wash it first with a disinfectant and scrub gently to remove any mould growth. Do not worry about any small chips – these will add to the aged effect.

You will need

Terracotta pot

Decorative stamping paint: yellow, cream, pale turquoise, mid-green, jade, brown and gold

Old 4cm (1½in) paintbrush

Small paintbrush

Applicator sponge and palette

Decorative stamp: ivy

Rubber solution glue

Powdered filler

Sawdust or clean sand

Tinted antiquing wax

2 soft lint-free cloths

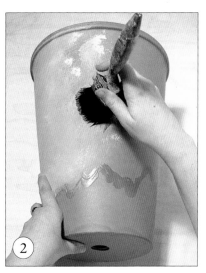

1. Paint a wiggly line of rubber solution glue approximately one fifth of the way up from the base of the pot. The more wiggly and jagged the line, the better.

2. Paint the section above the wiggly line using mid-green, pale turquoise, yellow and cream mixed on a 4cm (1½in) brush. Scrub the paint into the pot. Try to get subtle colour changes each time you reload the brush, and paint in random strokes. Leave to dry.

3. Mix up a paste using one part powdered filler, one part sawdust (or sand) and four parts water. Use the 4cm (1½in) paintbrush to apply this mixture to the lower section of the pot, under the glue line. Apply the paste in a stippling motion. Leave to dry.

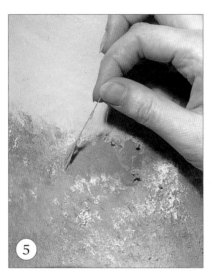

4. Stipple a mixture of mid-green, pale turquoise, brown and gold paint roughly on to the filler to create a verdigris effect. Leave to dry.

5. Peel off the rubber solution glue. You can use your finger to rub off any stubborn patches.

6. Blend mid-green and jade paint on an ivy stamp (see page 120). Press one end of the stamp on to the pot then carefully press along its length, taking care not to shift the image. Stamp around the top of the pot.

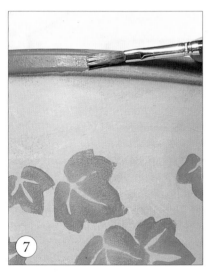

Note
If you find that you have a gap left around the pot that is not big enough for the whole ivy stamp, wash the stamp then apply paint to only one or two leaves to fill the space.

7. Paint a solid line of mid-green around the rim of the pot using a small paintbrush. Leave to dry.

8. Use a lint-free cloth to rub tinted antiquing wax all over the finished pot. Make sure you apply plenty of wax, and try to leave an uneven finish. Leave to dry for a few moments, then buff up with a clean lint-free cloth.

Note
You can make your own tinted wax by mixing a small amount of burnt sienna or raw umber oil paint with clear soft furniture wax. Wax can be corrosive, so any surplus mixture should be stored in a metal or glass container.

Terracotta pots

These pots are transformed using sun-drenched colours and they will brighten up any corner of your garden. A well-chosen stamp will make light work of decorating even a difficult curved surface. A layer of tinted wax will help protect your pot from the elements, but you may need to move the pot in winter as frost can be very damaging.

Mediterranean table

This unusual project uses an old table that is resurfaced to allow stamped tiles to be inset. To do this, simply lay your tiles on the old table top to create a border. Use matchsticks or pieces of thick card to space the tiles for grouting. Measure the rectangle in the centre and the border surrounding the tiles. Cut timber to these dimensions (a good DIY store will do this for you), remembering to use timber slightly thicker than your chosen tiles to allow for the adhesive beneath them. Alternatively, you could replace the tiles on a junk shop find.

Tile varnish will protect the stamped images, and make the table durable. Alternatively, use clear acrylic car lacquer.

You will need
Old table
Terracotta quarry tiles
Plywood
Acrylic decorative stamping
    paint: cream, red, yellow,
    mid-green, gold and brown
Decorative stamp: mosaic
    design
Clear air-drying tile varnish
6.5cm (2½in) old paintbrush
Applicator sponges and palette
Tile adhesive
Strong epoxy glue
Matchsticks
Grout
Grout spreader
Damp cloth

1. Decant pools of cream, brown, green and yellow paint onto a palette. Mix two parts paint to one part water. Blend together on the brush then apply this colourwash to each of the tiles. Leave to dry.

2. Use an applicator sponge to apply brown, red, yellow, mid-green and gold paint to the mosaic stamp. Blend the colours to soften the effect (see page 120). Stamp in all four corners of the tile. Leave to dry.

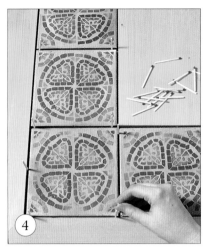

3. Stipple all over the tiles using air-drying tile varnish. Leave to dry for at least forty-eight hours. Repeat, then leave to dry again.

4. Spread tile adhesive into the area to be filled with tiles, then position the tiles using matchsticks or pieces of thick card for spacing. Leave to dry, following the manufacturer's instructions. Remove the spacers.

5. Follow the manufacturer's instructions to apply grout in between the tiles. Use a grout spreader to do this, and wipe the grout away from the edges of the tiles using a damp cloth.

Mediterranean table

Stamping is a quick and easy way to achieve an authentic-looking Mediterranean mosaic design. This table top has been transformed using painted and stamped terracotta tiles, and a wooden surround.

Primitive picture frame

Create three-dimensional stamped images by pressing a stamp into soft clay. Practice first, in order to gauge how hard you need to press to achieve a well-defined image. Air-hardening clay is the easiest to use but this may take up to forty-eight hours to dry, so check the manufacturer's instructions carefully before you start and allow yourself enough time to complete the project. This technique is also possible using fine papier mâché, oven-hardening clay or, if you have access to a kiln, regular clay.

You will need a piece of MDF for the backing of the frame and a piece of glass, cut and ground to the same size as your mount, to finish. Most good DIY stores will cut MDF, and you can ask your local framer or glass merchant to prepare the glass for you.

You will need
250g (½lb) air-hardening clay
Plain white paper
Old 4cm (1½in) brush
Decorative stamping paint: cream, brown, yellow and white
Decorative stamp: swirls
Applicator sponges and palette
Pale gold and copper gilding wax
MDF, 14cm (5½in) square, with a 9cm (3½in) square aperture
Glass, 8.5cm (3¼in) square
2 pieces of mount board, 8.5cm (3¼in) square
Photograph or picture
Ruler
Craft knife
Lint-free soft cloth
Glue and glue gun
25cm (10in) thin gold cord
Two lengths of scrap wood, approximately 1.5cm (½in) thick
Rolling pin
2.5cm (1in) masking tape

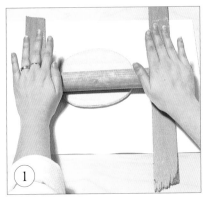

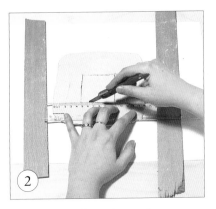

1. Place a piece of plain white paper on your work surface. Kneed the air-hardening clay until it is soft and smooth. Lay one length of scrap wood either side of the clay, then roll out the clay with a rolling pin. Use the pieces of wood as runners, to ensure that the clay has an even thickness all over.

2. Use your hands to shape a 16cm (6¼in) square. Measure in 5cm (2in) from all sides and then mark out a 6cm (2¼in) square in the middle. Use a ruler and a craft knife to cut out this aperture.

3. Position the swirls stamp over the clay, then press down firmly and evenly to leave an indentation. Repeat all over the frame. Do not allow the images to overlap. Leave to dry for at least forty-eight hours.

4. Load an old 4cm (1½in) paintbrush with dots of cream, brown, yellow and white paint. Dab the brush on to the side of the palette to mix the colours roughly. Stipple the paint all over the frame by dabbing the brush up and down. Try to get the paint down into the grooves. Leave to dry.

5. Use your finger to rub pale gold gilding wax into the raised pattern on the frame. Use the same technique and copper gilding wax to add highlights to other areas. Leave to dry for approximately five minutes before buffing up with a lint-free soft cloth.

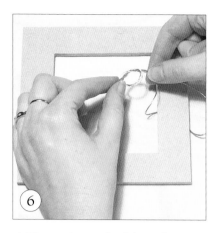

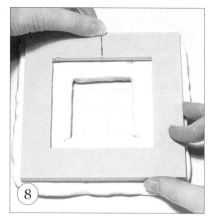

6. Tie a piece of gold cord around the top of the MDF. Position the knot centrally.

7. Use a glue gun to apply glue to the back of the frame.

8. Sandwich the knot between the MDF and the back of the frame. Hold in place for a few moments while the glue sets.

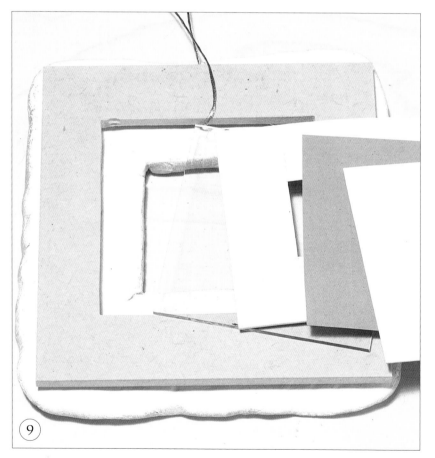

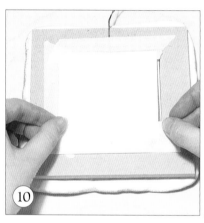

10. Tape the final piece of mount board securely in position using 2.5cm (1in) masking tape.

9. Place the glass in the aperture hole, then position the mount board. Now add a photograph or picture of your choice, and finally place another piece of mount board on top.

Primitive picture frame
Stamping in clay adds an
exciting dimension, giving deep
embossed effects. Gold and
copper gilding wax are used to
highlight the raised design,
which adds a warm sumptuous
glimmer. Adapt this technique to
make subtle baroque-style
mirrors, wall plaques, even
decorated matching plates or
bottles as shown here.

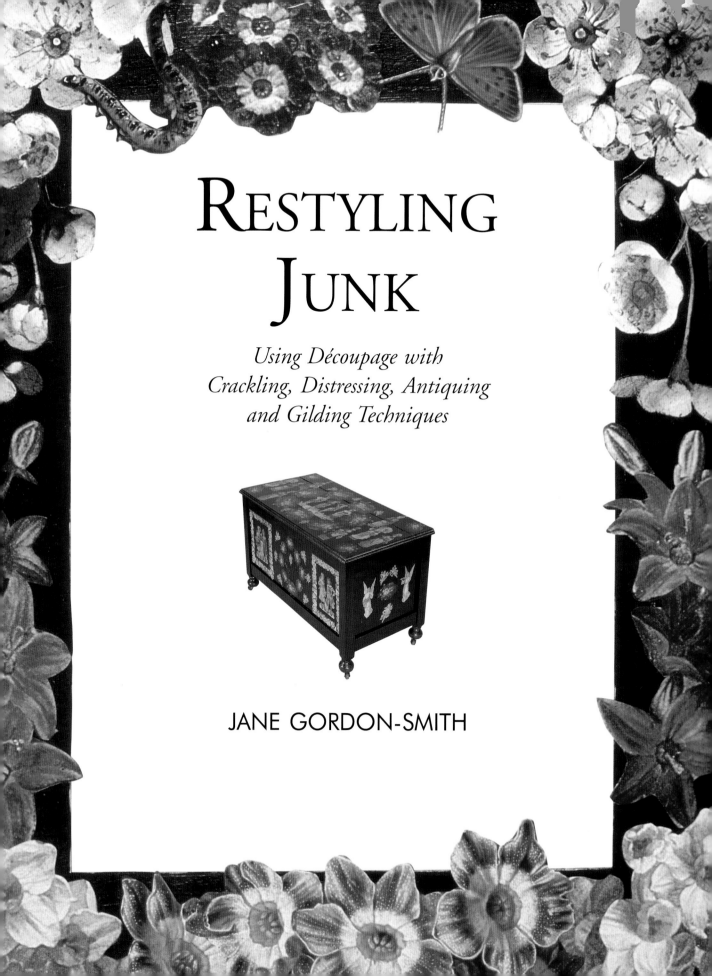

RESTYLING JUNK

Using Découpage with
Crackling, Distressing, Antiquing
and Gilding Techniques

JANE GORDON-SMITH

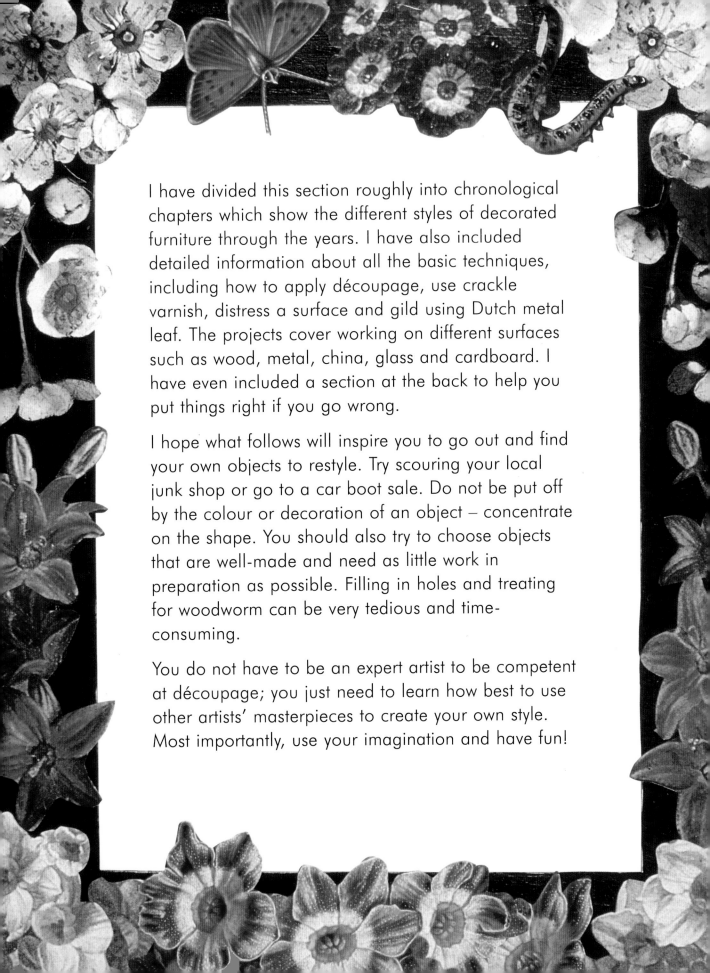

I have divided this section roughly into chronological chapters which show the different styles of decorated furniture through the years. I have also included detailed information about all the basic techniques, including how to apply découpage, use crackle varnish, distress a surface and gild using Dutch metal leaf. The projects cover working on different surfaces such as wood, metal, china, glass and cardboard. I have even included a section at the back to help you put things right if you go wrong.

I hope what follows will inspire you to go out and find your own objects to restyle. Try scouring your local junk shop or go to a car boot sale. Do not be put off by the colour or decoration of an object – concentrate on the shape. You should also try to choose objects that are well-made and need as little work in preparation as possible. Filling in holes and treating for woodworm can be very tedious and time-consuming.

You do not have to be an expert artist to be competent at découpage; you just need to learn how best to use other artists' masterpieces to create your own style. Most importantly, use your imagination and have fun!

MATERIALS

Listed below are the materials used for the paint effects, découpage and gilding shown in this book. They are all available from art and craft shops or hardware stores, and most newsagents stock gift wrap.

The materials required for each project are listed. In addition, you will need paper towelling for general mopping up, and white spirit and/or methylated spirit for cleaning brushes after use.

1. Water-based paints
Water-based emulsion paint can be used on most materials.

2. Artist's oil paints
Oil paint is used to show up the cracks when using the crackling technique. Burnt or raw Sienna or umber are the traditional colours used, but any coloured oil paint will work.

3. Watercolour paints
These are used to colour black and white photocopies.

4. Découpage paper and scraps
There is a huge selection of gift wrap available. Thin paper is better than thick. You can also buy images specially designed for découpage. Coloured or black and white photocopies are useful, particularly if you do not want to use an original piece such as a photograph.

5. Scissors
Small, sharp, pointed scissors are essential. I use straight-bladed scissors but some people find curved ones easier.

6. Brushes
Buy good quality varnish brushes and keep them exclusively for varnish. You will need one for water-based, one for oil-based and one for spirit-based varnish. You will also need a brush for paint and one for glue. The size of your brushes depends on the object to be decorated.

7. Chalk
Chalk is useful for marking the position of your design before gluing it in place.

8. Craft knife or scalpel
You can use a craft knife or scalpel for cutting out images, but I prefer to use scissors. A craft knife or scalpel is useful for cutting through a design to enable a box lid to open, for example, or to divide the panels of a screen. It is also used to remove bubbles under paper (see page 228).

9. Candle wax
This is used during the distressing technique, to artificially age a surface.

10. Metal primer
A commercial primer is available, designed for use specifically on metal.

11. Water-based gold size
A water-based gold size is used for sticking Dutch metal leaf on to a surface.

12. Methylated spirit
Brushes used with spirit-based products can be cleaned with methylated spirit.

13. White spirit
Brushes used with oil-based products can be cleaned with white spirit.

14. Sticky plastic (removable adhesive)
You will find sticky plastic useful for holding cut-outs in place on vertical objects prior to gluing them.

15. Wax polish
This is used for polishing a finished surface.

16. Gold, aluminium and copper Dutch metal leaf
These are used for gilding.

17. Metallic paints

Metallic paints can be used to fill in any small cracks that are left after gilding.

18. Wire wool

Very fine wire wool is used to apply wax polish. It can also be used to remove rust.

19. Duster

You will need a duster for polishing.

20. Cloth

A damp cloth is used to remove residue after sanding.

21. Paper towelling

Paper towelling is used to apply oil paint and for general mopping up.

22. Sandpaper

Use fine wet-and-dry sandpaper to rub down varnish in between coats. Medium and coarse grade sandpaper will be needed to prepare surfaces for painting and for distressing paint.

23. PVA Glue

PVA glue is suitable for découpage. For all projects in this book, a mixture of PVA glue and water should be used unless otherwise stated. The PVA glue should be diluted until it is the consistency of thin cream.

24. Sanding sealer

This is a clear spirit-based lacquer used for sealing crackle varnish. It can also be used in place of shellac, although it is clear in colour.

25. Oil-based varnish

Oil-based varnish is used after crackling and also if a really tough or heat-resistant finish is needed.

26. Water-based varnish

Use a quick-drying water-based acrylic varnish. This is readily available in hardware shops.

27. Shellac

Shellac is a spirit-based honey-coloured lacquer that is used for antiquing. French polish, white polish and knotting all belong to the same spirit-based family and can be used in place of shellac, although they all differ in colour. Sanding sealer can also be used, but it is clear-drying.

Shellac can be used to prime wood or cardboard. Commercial primers designed for use on specific materials are also available.

28. Crackle varnish

Two bottles of specialist varnish which together produce a crackled finish are available from art and craft shops. There are many different types, so read the instructions carefully. I use two-hour gold size as the undercoat and gum arabic solution as the top coat. The instructions for using these are shown on page 183.

29. Sponge

A damp sponge is useful when gluing.

30. Hairdryer

The crackling process involves the use of heat, and a hairdryer is ideal for this purpose.

These are the basic materials required for applying découpage with various decorative finishes. For more information about them, refer to pages 174–175.

1. Water-based paints

10. Metal primer

2. Artist's oil paints

3. Watercolour paints

4. Découpage paper and scraps

5. Scissors

8. Craft knife or scalpel

6. Brushes

7. Chalk

9. Candle wax

12. Methylated spirit

15. Wax polish

14. Sticky plastic

22. Sandpaper

11. Water-based gold size

21. Paper towelling

13. White spirit

20. Cloth

16. Gold, aluminium and copper Dutch metal leaf

18. Wire wool

19. Duster

17. Metallic paints

24. Sanding sealer

29. Sponge

27. Shellac

23. PVA glue

26. Water-based varnish

30. Hairdryer

25. Oil-based varnish

28. Crackle varnish

TECHNIQUES

Basic techniques

This section covers the basic techniques used in this book. The projects are all based on découpage which is not a difficult craft as it essentially involves just cutting out images, arranging a design and then gluing it in place. These techniques, although simple, do require time and patience. Careful cutting out is particularly important as it can make all the difference to a finished piece.

Cutting out

Cut around the image using a pair of small, sharp, pointed scissors. Move the paper and not the scissors. Make sure you cut away all the background, including any 'islands' of background in the middle of your design. To do this, pierce into the centre of the island with the tip of the scissors and then snip around it. If there are a lot of islands cut them out first, before the paper gets too flimsy.

Arranging a design

Move the paper cut-outs around until you are happy with the design. Pay attention to the shadows and do not put dark areas over light ones. Check that all the details are correct, for example that dew drops are dripping downwards and that insects are flying the right way up. When you are happy with the arrangement, glue in place with diluted PVA glue.

ABOVE
This photograph shows the wrong way to arrange a design. Notice how placing dark areas of images on top of light areas, creates an unnatural-looking design.

RIGHT
This photographs shows the design arranged correctly, with shaded areas underneath. If you compare it to the photograph above, you will see that this design looks more natural.

Working on a spherical surface

2. Stick the design on to a glass sphere using diluted PVA glue. Try to overlap the cuts to produce a natural-looking image.

NOTE

You can stick a design on to the outside of a glass container, or on to the inside (see page 223), depending on whether you want a functional or purely decorative piece.

1. Snip into the design at several points so that the paper will overlap itself when glued on to a spherical object. Always cut with the design. For example, if you are working on a flower, cut around petals.

Colouring a design

To colourwash a black and white photocopy, thin your paint with a little water. Choose a colour to complement the surface that it will be stuck on to. Brush the paint on quickly, and then immediately wipe it off with a damp sponge or some paper towelling. The image will now show through but the background will be coloured. When stuck on to a surface, the colourwashed design will look as if it has been drawn directly on.

NOTE

As an alternative to colourwashing, a black and white print can be painted with watercolour paints or pencils (see page 190).

An antique finish can be achieved by brushing on a thin coat of shellac over a coloured design (see the magazine rack on page 202).

Making a straight border

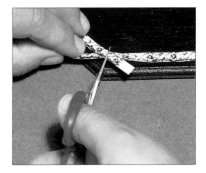

2. Where the borders cross at the corners, cut both pieces through the centre of the cross. Glue in place using diluted PVA glue.

1. Cut the border into strips roughly the same length as each edge, allowing for a small overlap. Place the strips on the object, with the corners overlapping. Paste the centre of each strip down using diluted PVA glue. Do not glue down the ends of each border strip.

Making a curved border

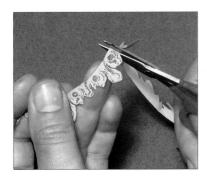

1. Make cuts into the border strips to enable them to be eased around a curve. Cut with the design, and snip almost up to the outside edge.

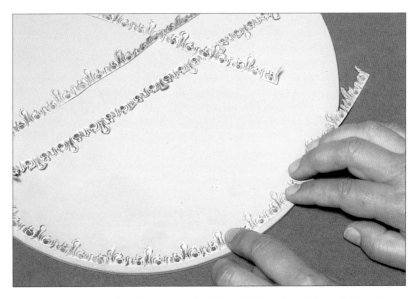

2. Paste the back of each strip with diluted PVA glue. Place the border on to your object. Ease it into position so that the cuts overlap naturally and the border forms into a curve.

Decorative finishes

Decorative finishes can add an extra dimension to painted or découpaged objects, and many have the effect of ageing an item. Here are some different finishes for you to try.

Distressed paint finish

The technique of distressing paint produces a soft, aged look and is particularly effective on a piece of furniture. Choose two colours of paint to go with your design or use just one colour over bare wood. The paint should be water-based emulsion. Here, pale blue is used under a cream top coat.

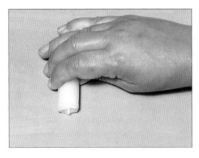 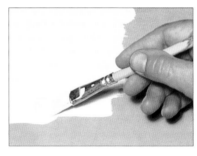 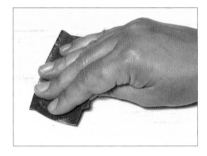

1. Paint the surface with the first colour and allow it to dry, or leave the wood bare. Rub candle wax over the surface, working with the grain. Pay particular attention to the areas that would distress naturally, such as handles or edges.

2. Brush a coat of the second colour over the wax. Brush in the direction of the grain. Allow to dry completely.

3. Rub the surface with a medium grade sandpaper. Again, work in the direction of the grain. The paint will rub off where there is wax underneath, leaving a distressed finish which can then be varnished or decorated with découpage.

This is a detail taken from the tray shown on page 185. The surface has been distressed, découpage has been applied, and the tray has then been crackled.

Crackling

There are many crackle varnishes available. They are all two-part varnishes and are applied one on top of the other. The bottom layer of varnish pulls the top layer apart to form cracks in the surface. I find that the most successful combination is an oil-based two-hour gold size as the first coat, and a water-based gum arabic solution as the second coat. As a general rule, a water-based product should not be applied over an oil-based product, but this is the exception to that rule.

1. Brush on a thin layer of two-hour gold size. Hold the article up to the light to check that the varnish is applied evenly and that it is covering the entire surface. Leave to dry in a cool, dry place for approximately one and a half hours, or until it is touch dry but still feels soft when pressed firmly with your finger.

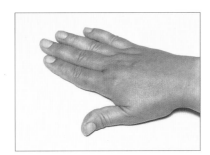

2. Brush on a coat of gum arabic solution. Use your hand to massage it into the bottom layer of varnish. Continue gently rubbing the surface for three to four minutes, or until the gum arabic begins to dry. Leave to dry naturally for at least two hours, but preferably overnight.

3. Use a hairdryer to gently heat the varnish for a couple of minutes. This process will cause the cracks to form, but at this stage they will barely show up.

4. Mix some artist's oil paint with a little white spirit until it is the consistency of toothpaste. Rub the thinned paint into the varnished surface using paper towelling.

5. Use a clean piece of paper towelling to wipe off all the excess paint, leaving colour only in the cracks. Leave to dry for about twelve hours. Seal with an oil- or spirit-based varnish.

Dutch metal gilding

Dutch metal leaf comes in three basic colours: gold, aluminium (silver) and copper (bronze). It can be bought as loose leaf or transfer leaf; the latter comes with a backing paper and is used in this example. The leaf adheres to water-based gold size. Once you have brushed on the size, the leaf must be applied within six hours.

> **NOTE**
>
> A coat of either red or black emulsion paint should be used underneath gold leaf. Blue works best underneath aluminium, and terracotta or green underneath copper.
>
> Metal leaf can be sealed with water- or spirit-based varnish. Shellac can also be used, but remember that this will alter the colour of the metal leaf.

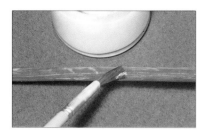

1. Paint your item with a base coat of emulsion and allow to dry. Brush the size on to the areas you want to gild.

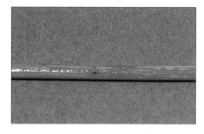

2. Leave to dry for at least five minutes, or until the size goes clear.

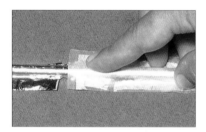

3. Cut the transfer leaf and backing paper into sizes suitable for your item. Carefully place each piece metal side down on to the clear size. Smooth over the backing paper with your fingers to transfer the leaf to the item. Gently peel away the backing paper. Repeat with the next piece of leaf, overlapping the first slightly. Continue until all the size is covered. Leave to dry for at least one hour.

4. Smooth over the metal leaf using a piece of cotton wool.

5. Brush off excess leaf using a soft paintbrush. Fill in any cracks using metallic paint, and use size and leftover leaf for any big holes. Seal with water- or spirit-based varnish.

> **NOTE**
>
> There are a number of metallic paints available which you can use as an alternative to Dutch metal leaf. The paints can be applied with a small paintbrush as shown opposite. Gold and silver felt-tip pens can also be used, but do try them out first on a piece of paper and make sure the various varnishes will not cause them to run or change colour.

A rich design of roses was applied on top of a distressed painted background to produce this classic bed tray. The tray was then given six layers of water-based varnish, before crackle varnish was applied. Burnt sienna oil paint was rubbed in to reveal the cracks. Three coats of oil-based polyurethane varnish were then applied, and the tray was finished with wax polish.

This collection of objects shows various decorative finishes, and all of the items use either Dutch metal leaf or metallic paint.

The oval trinket box was covered with Dutch metal gold leaf and then découpaged.

The green playing card box was distressed and then borders and a photocopy of a lion's head were colourwashed and stuck in place. Antique gold paint was then applied around the lid.

The table mat was découpaged and a border was then painted on with antique gold paint.

REPRODUCTION
CHINESE
LACQUERWORK

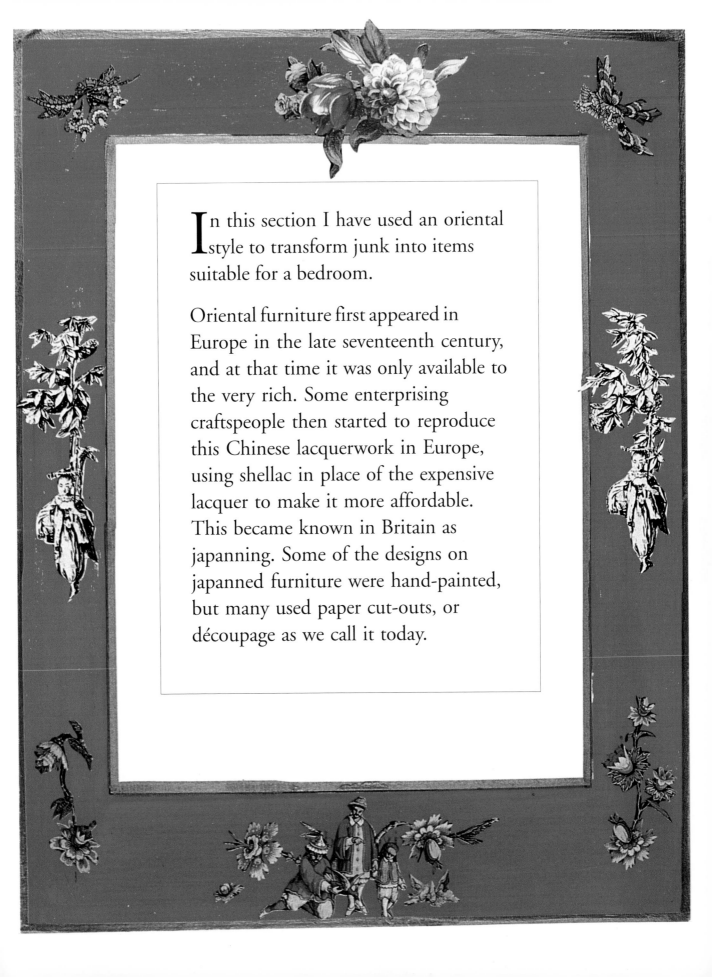

In this section I have used an oriental style to transform junk into items suitable for a bedroom.

Oriental furniture first appeared in Europe in the late seventeenth century, and at that time it was only available to the very rich. Some enterprising craftspeople then started to reproduce this Chinese lacquerwork in Europe, using shellac in place of the expensive lacquer to make it more affordable. This became known in Britain as japanning. Some of the designs on japanned furniture were hand-painted, but many used paper cut-outs, or découpage as we call it today.

This is the collection of junk before transformation. Turn to pages 192–195 to see how these items have been dramatically improved.

Bamboo table

A bamboo table was an ideal subject to transform using an oriental theme. I had intended to paint the legs to match the top, but having applied a coat of shellac as a primer, I then changed my mind as the bamboo looked lovely in its natural state. Spirit-based products, such as shellac, make ideal primers (particularly if you are unsure what the surface is underneath) as both oil and water-based products can be used over them.

1. Remove the beading from the table top. Sand down the table using a medium grade sandpaper. If the surface is very rough, begin with a coarse grade. Wrap the sandpaper around a sanding block to do large flat areas.

2. Remove any debris with a damp cloth. Allow to dry. Brush shellac over the entire table.

3. Paint the table top and bottom shelf with black emulsion. Allow to dry. Sand lightly with fine wet-and-dry sandpaper. Remove any debris with a damp cloth. Apply a coat of red emulsion. Leave to dry.

4. Apply gold leaf to the beading (see page 184). Use the No. 6 paintbrush to apply the size. Glue the beading back on to the table top using undiluted PVA glue. Tack the beading firmly in place using small panel pins.

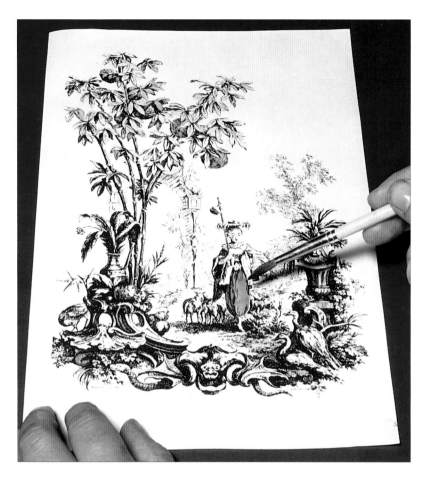

5. Colour photocopied designs using watercolour paints and a No. 6 paintbrush. It does not matter if you go over some of the edges of the design. Leave to dry and then cut the images out (see page 178).

6. Arrange the images on the table top and the bottom shelf. When you are happy with the arrangement, mark the position of some of the points of the design with chalk.

7. Paste all over the back of the image with diluted PVA glue. Use the chalk marks as a guide to position the design back on the table top and bottom shelf.

8. Press out any wrinkles or air bubbles with a damp sponge and wipe away any remaining chalk marks. Leave to dry.

 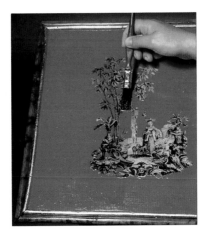 

9. Paint the table top and bottom shelf with water-based varnish. Leave to dry and then repeat until you have built up six layers in total. Lightly sand with wet-and-dry sandpaper then remove any debris with a damp cloth. Allow to dry.

10. Paint the table top and bottom shelf with shellac. Allow to dry completely before applying a second coat. Repeat, building up the coats of shellac until you have the colour finish you like (this can be anything between two and ten coats). Leave to dry completely.

11. Sand the table top and bottom shelf with wet-and-dry sandpaper to remove any impurities from the surface. Remove any debris with a damp cloth. Apply a coat of oil-based varnish. Leave to dry overnight.

12. Apply wax polish to the table top, bottom shelf and legs using wire wool. Rub it in well.

13. Buff off the polish with a clean duster.

The finished bamboo table looks stunning alongside this matching table lamp.

The lamp base was gilded and then antiqued with shellac to enhance the colour of the gold. The lamp shade was then painted red, the edges were gilded and a final coat of water-based varnish was applied to complete the transformation.

This pretty jewellery box was a badly rusted tin before it was transformed. It was treated with a rust remover before being painted with red oxide primer and red emulsion paint. The flowers were stuck on and the whole box was then varnished in the same way as the table (see page 191).

The cut-out flowers on this sphere have all been stuck on to the inside of the glass. As the aperture is very small, a piece of damp cloth was tied to the end of a paintbrush to smooth the design into place. The inside was then painted with two shades of yellow paint to give a mottled look to the finished object.

This miniature papier-mâché trunk was given two coats of cream emulsion paint and then the features were picked out in pale blue. A willow pattern was applied and the surface was crackled to create a porcelain effect.

This impressive tray was created by first applying a coat of red oxide primer followed by a coat of black emulsion paint. The Chinese motif was applied to the centre and the edges were worked in antique gold paint. Water-based varnish was applied and then layers of oil-based polyurethane varnish were built up to provide a tough, heat-resistant finish.

This spectacular bed shows just how effective découpage can be, and how brilliantly it can transform an object. The headboard and footboard were sanded down and painted with two coats of black emulsion. The edges were then given a coat of red emulsion and gilded with gold Dutch metal transfer leaf. The découpage was added, then two coats of water-based varnish were applied. Eight coats of shellac were built up to deepen the colour and produce a rich effect. The bed was given two coats of oil-based varnish and finished off with wax polish.

This detail is taken from the inside of the footboard and shows the exquisite gift wrap used for this project. The large flower design looks very effective against the black background.

GEORGIAN
ELEGANCE

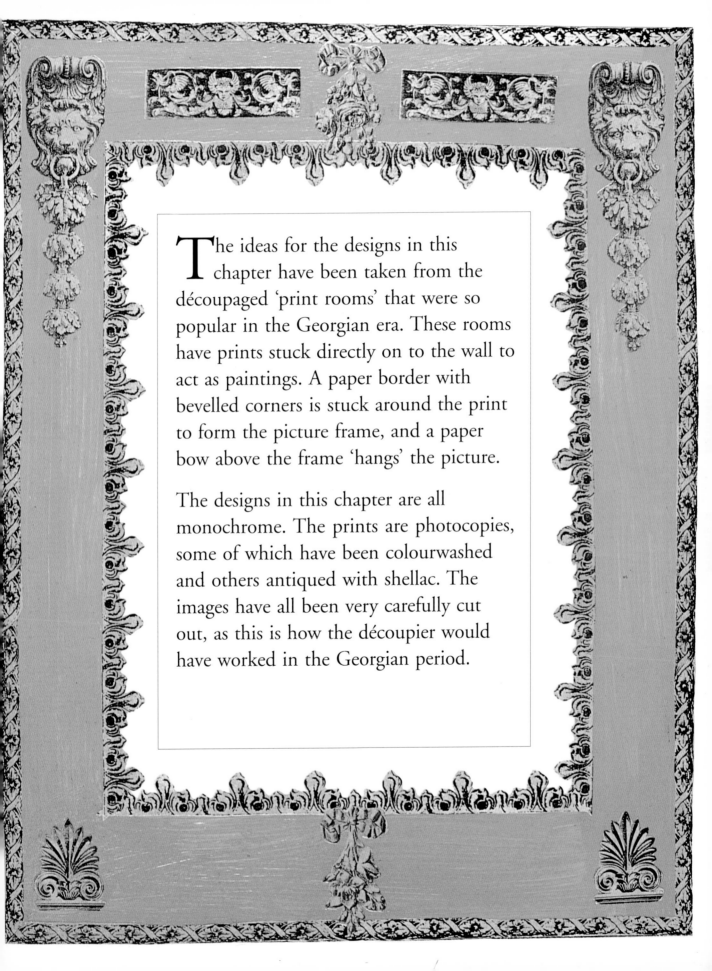

The ideas for the designs in this chapter have been taken from the découpaged 'print rooms' that were so popular in the Georgian era. These rooms have prints stuck directly on to the wall to act as paintings. A paper border with bevelled corners is stuck around the print to form the picture frame, and a paper bow above the frame 'hangs' the picture.

The designs in this chapter are all monochrome. The prints are photocopies, some of which have been colourwashed and others antiqued with shellac. The images have all been very carefully cut out, as this is how the découpier would have worked in the Georgian period.

All the items in this collection of junk are well made, but tatty. They can be dramatically transformed using gilding, crackling, distressing and découpage techniques to create stunning new looks (see pages 200–203).

China plate

I bought this plain white china plate because of its unusual shape. I thought that, when decorated, it would be useful to have on the hall table for keys. The method shown here for painting and découpaging the china plate can be used on any ceramics, including tiles.

YOU WILL NEED

China plate
Medium grade sandpaper
PVA glue
Emulsion paint: black
Photocopied print and border design
Water-based varnish
Crackle varnish: two-hour gold size and gum arabic solution
Hairdryer
Artist's oil paint: burnt umber and cream
Three 2.5cm (1in) paintbrushes for paint, water-based varnish and oil-based varnish
Glue brush
Sponge
Paper towelling
White spirit
Damp cloth

1. Wash the plate in warm soapy water to remove any grease or dirt. Rub it down with a medium grade sandpaper to create a key. Remove any debris with a damp cloth.

2. Brush on a thin coat of diluted PVA glue and leave to dry.

3. Paint the plate with black emulsion. Leave to dry. Apply a second coat. Leave to dry.

4. Arrange the design and the border on the plate, and then glue it in place (see page 181). Leave the glue to dry. Apply a coat of water-based varnish.

6. Brush on a coat of oil-based varnish to finish the plate.

5. Apply oil- and water-based crackle varnish to the plate (see page 183). Use cream oil paint to bring up the crackle on the black sections of the design, and dark brown to bring up the crackle on the white sections (see page 183).

The finished plate looks impressive, and can be used as a decorative or functional item. The final coat of oil-based varnish provides a protective finish, and the plate can be washed gently in warm soapy water. It must not, however, be put it in the dishwasher.

It is hard to believe that this plate is made of glass not gold! To create this illusion, a black and white antiqued design was applied to the underside of the plate, and it was then gilded. Water- then oil-based varnish were then applied over the gold metal leaf to make it durable. The finished plate can be washed gently in warm soapy water.

This mirror was in a poor state originally. The frame was cracked and had to be filled with wood filler, and the whole frame was rubbed down with medium grade sandpaper. It was then primed with sanding sealer, gilded with aluminium leaf and decorated with pale blue colourwashed prints. Finally, three coats of shellac were applied, giving the golden bronze colour.

The candlesticks were decorated using a black and white print coloured with French polish. The print was a photocopy of a piece of mock leopard skin fabric.

This little Italian-style trinket box has been given a new lease of life. The flower design was cut out very carefully and the intricate border was placed precisely. Crackle varnish was used to complete the transformation.

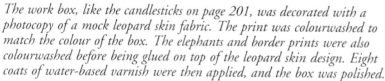

The work box, like the candlesticks on page 201, was decorated with a photocopy of a mock leopard skin fabric. The print was colourwashed to match the colour of the box. The elephants and border prints were also colourwashed before being glued on top of the leopard skin design. Eight coats of water-based varnish were then applied, and the box was polished.

OPPOSITE
This table looks dramatically different now. The transformation began by applying a pale blue undercoat. A cream top coat was painted on and it was then distressed. A black and white photocopied design was colourwashed cream and applied around the border and legs.

The magazine rack has a musical theme. The prints were coloured with French polish before being cut out and applied. Water-based varnish was then applied and the rack was finished with French polish.

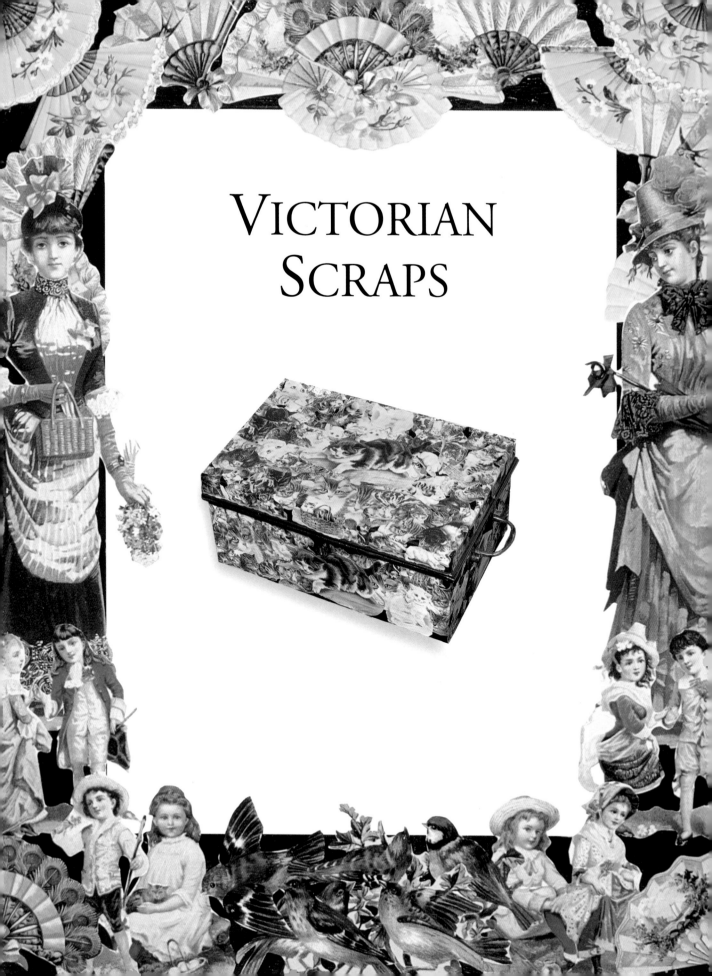

VICTORIAN
SCRAPS

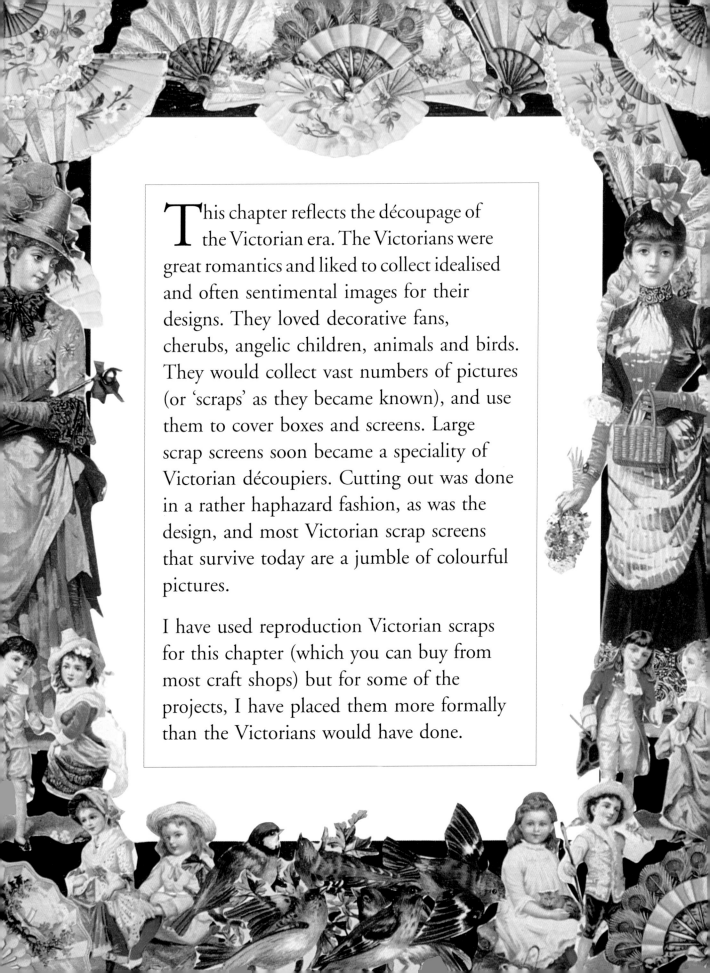

This chapter reflects the découpage of the Victorian era. The Victorians were great romantics and liked to collect idealised and often sentimental images for their designs. They loved decorative fans, cherubs, angelic children, animals and birds. They would collect vast numbers of pictures (or 'scraps' as they became known), and use them to cover boxes and screens. Large scrap screens soon became a speciality of Victorian découpiers. Cutting out was done in a rather haphazard fashion, as was the design, and most Victorian scrap screens that survive today are a jumble of colourful pictures.

I have used reproduction Victorian scraps for this chapter (which you can buy from most craft shops) but for some of the projects, I have placed them more formally than the Victorians would have done.

Here is the collection of junk before being transformed using the Victorian style of découpage. Turn to pages 208–211 to see how these items can be given striking face lifts.

Metal cash box

Metal is an easy material to découpage, and it is often very rewarding to work on as its transformation can be so startling. Metal trunks and boxes can be found in most junk shops. The old cash box featured in this project was in a good condition when I bought it, but do not be put off if you come across something that is rusted or dented. This need not matter as the rust can be removed easily with rust remover; and the dents, if not too big, can add to the appeal of the finished object, particularly if given an antique finish.

1. Sand down the box using coarse grade sandpaper or wire wool. This will remove any rust or flaking paint and give the surface a key. If your box is badly rusted, use a rust remover first. Remove any debris with a damp cloth.

2. Paint the box with red oxide primer and leave to dry.

3. Apply a coat of black emulsion to the box. Leave to dry before applying a second coat. Again, leave to dry.

4. Paste cut-out cats on to the box using diluted PVA glue. Paint over the entire box with diluted PVA glue, making sure that all the edges are stuck down. Leave to dry completely.

NOTE

Try to cover the box completely, positioning the cats so that they face in all directions. I try to finish by placing one large cat on the centre of each surface to act as a focal point.

NOTE

Always allow the shellac to dry completely between coats to prevent a sticky mess accumulating.

Shellac is quite hard-wearing, but if your object is going to be used a lot, you could apply one or two coats of oil-based varnish on top of the shellac to give an even tougher protective finish.

5. Apply a coat of water-based varnish. Leave to dry before applying a second coat. Leave to dry.

6. Apply two or more coats of shellac, depending on how dark an antique finish you want (see page 191). Leave to dry thoroughly between coats.

This tin box looks splendid covered entirely with scraps, and is perfect for cat lovers! The box has a shelf inside, so it could be used on a large desk to store pens and paper.

Blanket boxes are always useful and can usually be found quite cheaply. This blanket box has been decorated using Victorian scraps arranged in a more formal style than the Victorians themselves would have worked. It was sanded down and painted with black emulsion paint. The edge of the lid and the feet were painted with antique gold paint and the design was then applied to the front and side panels and the top. It was varnished with eight layers of water-based varnish and finished off with two coats of oil-based varnish.

The round papier mâché box was découpaged and given a crackle finish to transform it into a lovely Victorian-style sewing box. The oil lamp was painted with red oxide primer and the Victorian scraps were applied directly on to this base. Coats of water-based followed by oil-based varnish were applied, making it suitable for use both indoors and outdoors.

A glass bowl has here been totally transformed. All the work has been done on the outside, which means that it can now be used as a decorative or functional item. The plain glass surface was crackled, and the varnish was sealed with clear-drying sanding sealer. The clowns were glued on, facing inwards. The bowl was then painted with green emulsion and gilded with copper Dutch metal leaf. Another set of clowns were stuck on, facing outwards. Water-based varnish was applied, followed by two coats of oil-based varnish. The finished bowl can be washed gently in warm soapy water.

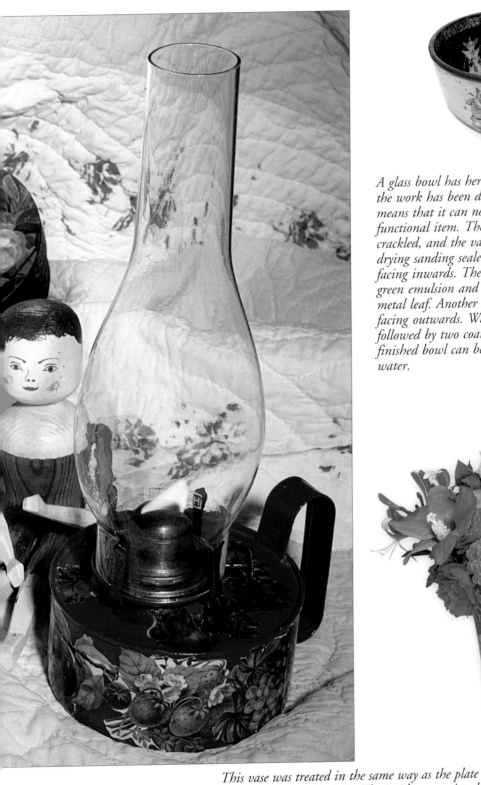

This vase was treated in the same way as the plate featured on pages 199–200. The inside was painted and oil-based varnish was applied over water-based varnish, so the finished vase will hold water.

POST
VICTORIAN
DESIGNS

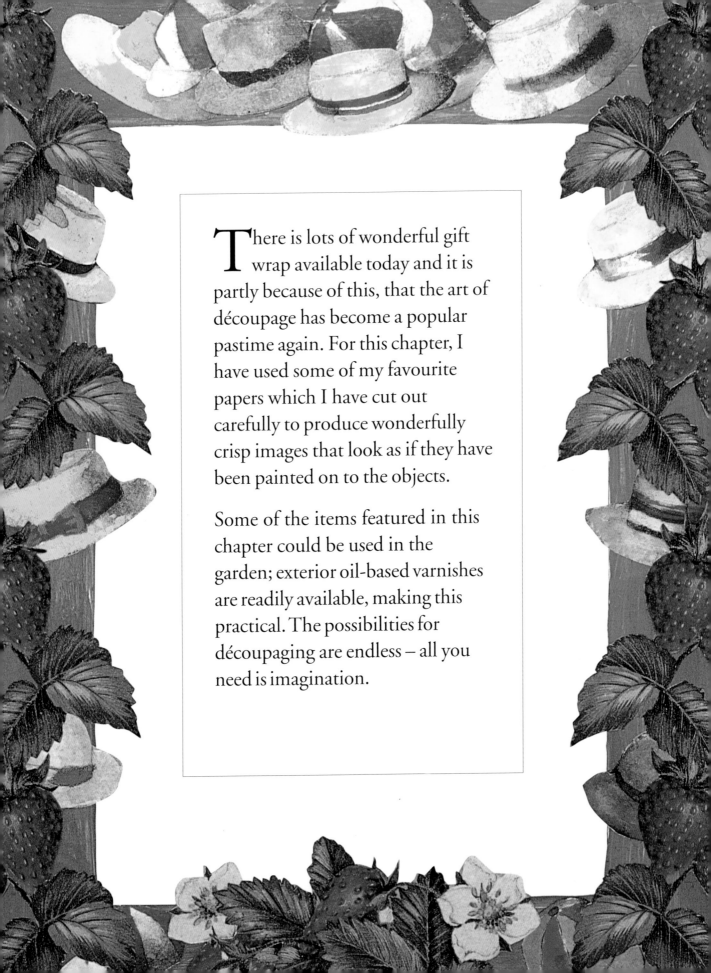

There is lots of wonderful gift wrap available today and it is partly because of this, that the art of découpage has become a popular pastime again. For this chapter, I have used some of my favourite papers which I have cut out carefully to produce wonderfully crisp images that look as if they have been painted on to the objects.

Some of the items featured in this chapter could be used in the garden; exterior oil-based varnishes are readily available, making this practical. The possibilities for découpaging are endless – all you need is imagination.

This disparate-looking collection of junk can be dramatically improved and turned into objects suitable for use in the conservatory and garden. Turn to pages 215-219 to see how effective this transformation can be.

Cardboard box

The cardboard box shown in this chapter was once the packaging for a Christmas present.
It was in good condition and so instead of painting it with water-based emulsion, I left it
as it was and decorated it using large, richly coloured roses.

YOU WILL NEED

Cardboard box
Flowery gift wrap
Small, sharp, pointed scissors
PVA glue
Water-based varnish
2.5cm (1in) paintbrush
Glue brush

1. Cut out the flowers from gift
wrap, being careful to cut away all
the islands of background (see
page 178). Arrange your design
on the box, making sure that the
images on the sides will not be
obscured when the lid is in place.
Paste images on to all four sides
of the box and the top of the lid
using diluted PVA glue.

2. Glue smaller cut-out images
around the side of the box lid to
form a border. Make sure that the
corner pieces are well stuck down
to give a sharp edge. Leave to dry.
Apply a coat of water-based
varnish to the entire box. Leave
to dry completely before applying
a second coat.

*The finished cardboard box can now be used as a very pretty
storage container. Lots of packaging is suitable for
decorating. Soaps, playing cards and many other items come
in wonderful boxes, many of which cry out for a new look.*

The kettle was treated in the same way as the cash box featured on pages 207–208 and will now make a wonderful watering can for indoor plants.

Terracotta flower pots can be turned into very decorative items. The pots at the front were sealed with PVA, one was painted with cream emulsion and the other left plain. The pots were then découpaged and given two coats of water-based varnish.

The ceramic pot at the back was treated in the same way as the plate on page 199.

The paraffin heater was treated with a rust remover and then sanded down. It was given a coat of red oxide primer, painted cream and the edges and detail were then picked out in green. It was decorated with strawberries and given four coats of water-based varnish to finish.

This pretty table was crackled and decorated with a wreath of flowers and butterflies. The butterflies were cut out very carefully, making sure that the antennae remained intact. The details on the legs were then picked out in green. The table was finished with water-based varnish followed by two coats of oil-based exterior varnish, making it weatherproof and therefore suitable for use in the garden.

Opposite

This zinc bath was treated with a metal primer, painted with emulsion and then decorated with cut-out strawberries. It was then finished with four coats of water-based varnish, followed by two coats of oil-based exterior varnish, making it weatherproof. It could now be planted with flowers or even strawberries, or tubs of herbs could be placed in it.

Look out in your local junk shops for old zinc baths, watering cans and jugs. Make sure they do not leak if you want to use them, and remember to remove all rust before you apply a metal primer.

DEVELOPING
a THEME

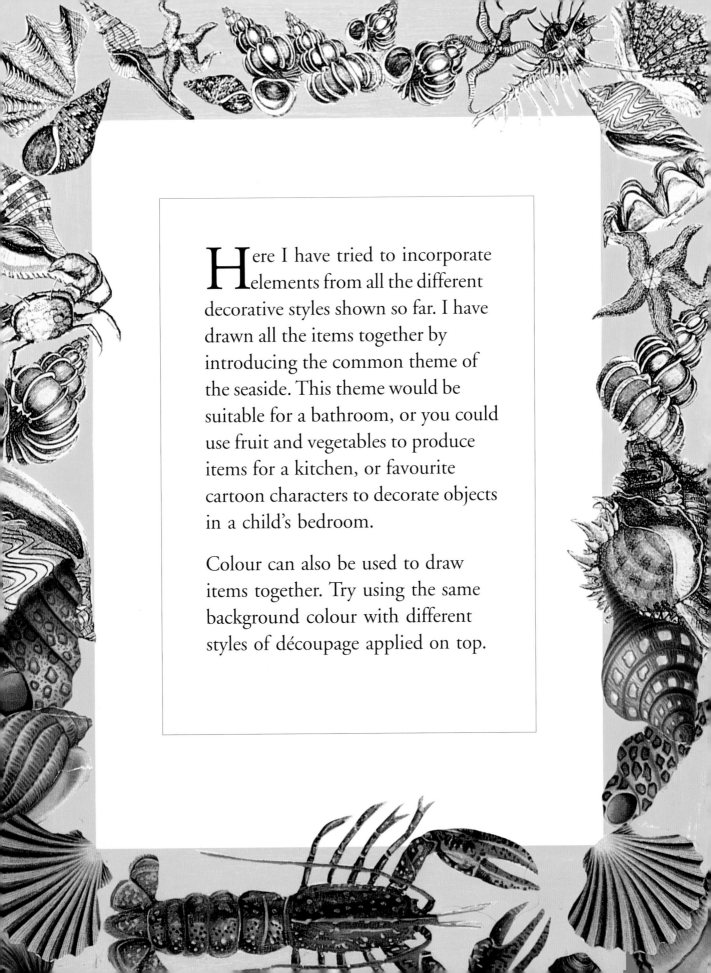

Here I have tried to incorporate elements from all the different decorative styles shown so far. I have drawn all the items together by introducing the common theme of the seaside. This theme would be suitable for a bathroom, or you could use fruit and vegetables to produce items for a kitchen, or favourite cartoon characters to decorate objects in a child's bedroom.

Colour can also be used to draw items together. Try using the same background colour with different styles of découpage applied on top.

Glass jar

The technique of decorating the inside of a glass object involves working in reverse: you apply the découpage first, then the paint. The inside of the jar is varnished, but the glass itself acts as the varnish for the outside. When choosing an item of glassware for this technique, make sure the gap at the top is big enough to get your hand into.
For this project, you can use a photocopier to alter the size of the images and thereby create small and large fish and shells.

YOU WILL NEED

Glass jar

Fish and shell photocopies in various sizes

Small, sharp, pointed scissors

PVA glue

Damp cloth

Water-based gold size

Dutch metal aluminium leaf

Metallic silver paint

Emulsion paint: yellow

Water-based varnish

Three 2.5cm (1in) paint-brushes for paint, water-based varnish and aluminium leaf (a soft, dry one should be used for the aluminium leaf)

Two 1cm (1/2in) paintbrushes for glue and size

No. 6 paintbrush for silver paint

1. Cut out the photocopied images (see page 12). Paste the right side of each image with diluted PVA glue and then stick them on to the inside of the glass jar. Gently wipe over the images with a damp cloth.

2. Paint the whole of the inside of the jar with diluted PVA glue. Check that all the edges are stuck down. Allow to dry.

NOTE

If you want to check your design before sticking, use some sticky plastic to stick your images on to the outside of the jar and transfer to the inside when gluing.

When sticking images on to glass, press out all the air bubbles with your fingers as they will show through the glass. Make sure all the edges are stuck down before wiping over the whole surface with a damp cloth.

OPPOSITE
This is the plain collection of junk before transformation. Turn to pages 224–227 to see how these items can be dramatically improved and made suitable for use in the bathroom.

3. Apply size carefully to the inside rim of the jar. Leave to dry for at least five minutes or until the size goes clear (see page 184).

4. Apply the aluminium transfer leaf to the clear size to cover the rim (see page 184). Leave to dry for at least two hours and then brush away the excess with a soft, dry brush.

5. Use a small paintbrush and silver paint to fill in any cracks on the rim. If there are any large holes, fill them in with size and any leftover aluminium leaf. Leave to dry.

6. Apply a coat of yellow emulsion to the inside of the jar. Leave to dry before applying a second coat. When that is dry, apply two coats of water-based varnish, again allowing time to dry between coats.

The finished jar looks splendid and is perfect for storing soap or cotton wool in the bathroom. The lid has been left plain, but you could choose to decorate it to match the jar.

The tiles on this page were originally all different colours. The orange tile on the right was left unpainted, but the others were decorated to match each other. Tiles can be treated in the same way as the china plate featured on pages 199–200. You can decorate tiles either on or off the wall, giving countless possibilities for redecorating. Before you begin, remember to wash the tiles in warm soapy water to remove any grease or soap. This is particularly important if you are decorating tiles on a wall in the kitchen or bathroom.

This chair has been decorated to create a very personal piece of découpage. It was first sanded down, then the details on the legs and back were painted with black emulsion. When dry, antique gold paint was applied. The rest of the chair was left unpainted so that it could be covered with photocopies of three generations of my family on seaside holidays. The Victorian style of placing pictures in all directions and almost one on top of the other was used. The chair was given a coat of water-based varnish, followed by four coats of shellac to create a sepia look. Finally, three coats of oil-based varnish were applied. To create a black and white effect (see the Victorian hat box opposite), you can use water-based varnish in place of shellac.

This charming candle holder has been painted pale yellow and covered with colourwashed photocopies of coral. A coat of water-based varnish was then applied. It has not been crackled, but a little burnt umber artist's oil paint was rubbed into the corners to antique it. A layer of oil-based varnish was then applied.

This old Victorian hat box has been decorated with my family snaps in a Georgian style. Water-based varnish was used in place of shellac to ensure that the images remained black and white. Photographs can be used to great effect with découpage. You could use black and white or colour photocopies of wedding or christening photographs, for example, to create a very special commemorative piece. The service sheet and invitation could also be incorporated into the design.

This scoop was painted with a metal primer and blue emulsion paint. The colourful cut-out sea creatures were then glued on and five coats of water-based varnish were applied.

PUTTING WRONGS RIGHT

Everyone makes mistakes, however long they have been doing découpage. In fact, I have a house full of slight seconds that cannot be sold on to the trade! Most problems occur at the gluing stage, although using crackle varnish can also be problematic. Here are some of the more common mistakes and how to correct them.

Cutting away part of your design

This is easily rectified. Cut out all the elements of the design that you need and then at the gluing stage, simply fit them all together like a jigsaw puzzle. By the time you have finished varnishing, you will not see the joins.

Bubbles and bumps under the paper

If, once you have stuck on your design and allowed it to dry completely, you find bubbles of air trapped under the paper, cut though the bubble using a craft knife or scalpel. Try to get the cut working with an element in the design if possible. For instance, if the bubble is over a flower, cut along the line of a petal. Push a little PVA glue into the cut, then press down with your finger to push out the air and stick down the paper. The paper may overlap at the cut, which is why it is best to cut with the design if possible.

Some bumps may have glue rather than air in them. This occurs when the PVA glue mixture is too thick. Unfortunately, the problem cannot be rectified, but you should remember to dilute the PVA glue a little more when working on your next project.

Tearing the paper when gluing

When paper is wet with PVA glue, it tears easily. If you find that a particular paper is thin and tears easily, brush on a coat of sanding sealer to strengthen the paper. Leave to dry before cutting out.

Be careful when placing your design and do not rub the paper too hard when pushing out air bubbles. If the paper does tear, push it back together and glue it in place. If you find that there is a white edge to the tear once the glue has dried, use watercolour paints to mix up a colour that will match the design, then dab a little on to the tear. If the tear is big and you cannot push it back together, add a bit of extra design to cover it, such as a butterfly or a flower.

Breaking through the paper when sanding down the varnish

This will cause an unsightly white mark. Mix up a matching colour using watercolour paints. Dab the paint on to the white spot on the paper, then wipe it off with a piece of paper towelling. The watercolour paint will soak into the bare paper, but it will wipe away from the varnished areas. Allow the paint to dry, and then apply another coat of varnish. To prevent breaking the paper in future, do not attempt to sand until you have applied at least five coats of varnish.

Crackle varnish

Crackle varnish can be temperamental, particularly if used in extremes of heat, cold or humidity, so always try to apply crackle varnish in a moderate temperature.

If, after having shown up the cracks with artist's oil paint, there are one or two blotches that look unattractive, remove them with the corner of a piece of paper towelling dipped in a little white spirit. This will remove the oil paint and therefore hide the mistake. If, you are unhappy with the overall effect, remove all the oil paint using paper towelling soaked in white spirit. Seal the crackle varnish with sanding sealer then begin the crackling process again.

If the crackle varnish has wrinkles in it, this cannot be corrected. It is caused by the first coat of varnish being applied too thickly. Remember to apply it more thinly next time. If it has thickened in the jar, thin it by adding a small amount of white spirit.

Do not forget that crackle varnish must be sealed with a spirit- or oil-based varnish. Water-based products will remove the gum arabic solution and the cracks will therefore disappear as well.

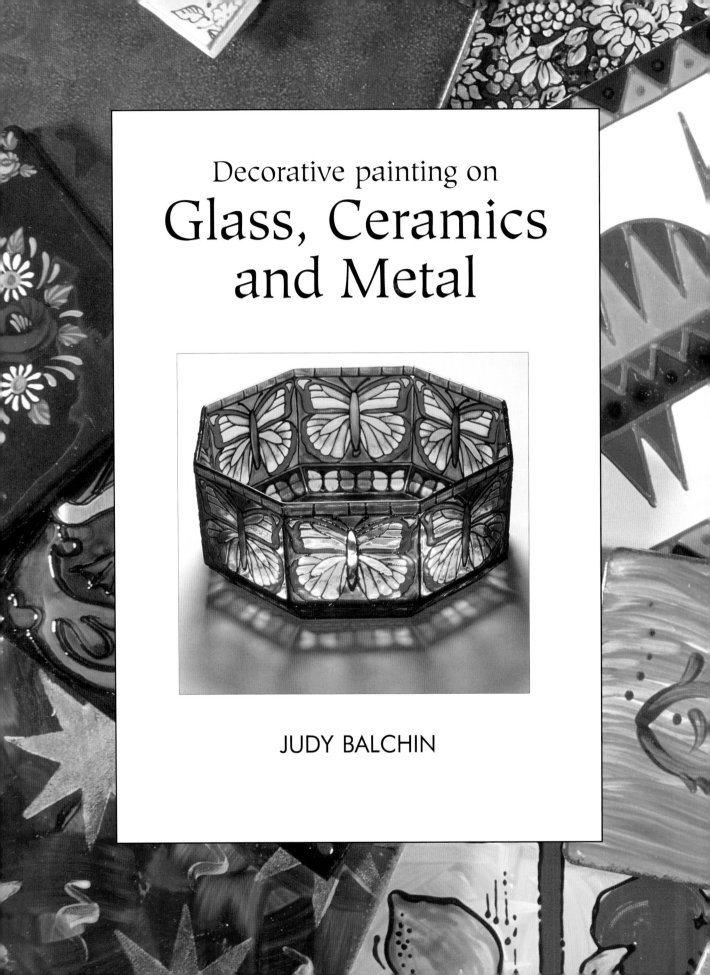

Decorative painting on
Glass, Ceramics and Metal

JUDY BALCHIN

Painted and decorated china, glass and metalware have always fascinated me. I love visiting antique and junk shops. There, I can absorb the wonderful patterns and images created by craftsmen and women throughout the years. This has, however, been quite a frustrating pastime . . . until recently. I had often wondered how I could reproduce that professional finish without the aid of a kiln, and without the knowledge of the different glazes used for decoration. Then, to my delight, I discovered a whole range of paints that could be applied to china, glass and metal which did not require firing in a kiln. These paints can be applied to any smooth surface, they are durable and give a truly professional finish.

This discovery has opened up a whole new exciting world for me. I can now create my own designs, or paint items to match existing surroundings and decor. I still browse around antique and junk shops, but I also visit charity and kitchen shops, hunting for inexpensive and original pieces to paint – items with pleasing or unusual shapes which could be enhanced by decoration.

Pieces can be painted to match your decor, personalised to provide a perfect gift, or simply decorated for fun. Whatever you choose to transform, I hope you enjoy creating something unique.

Materials

All the materials and equipment used in this book are readily available from art and craft suppliers, DIY stores, stationers and supermarkets, and you may even already have many of the items in your own home. As you work with the paints you will find yourself inventing new uses for ordinary everyday materials such as absorbent paper, cotton buds, cocktail sticks and sponges – these can all be put to good use. A comprehensive list of all the materials and equipment needed for every project featured in this book is provided on page 236.

Keep your eyes open for items to decorate. Junk shops and charity shops provide a rich source, along with kitchen, homeware and DIY outlets. Odd cups, saucers and teapots can be painted with the same decoration to form a new, coordinated tea set (see page 279). So, search those kitchen cupboards, collect old bottles and jars (especially ones with unusual shapes) and do not throw anything away!

Paints

All the paints used in this book are specially designed to adhere to smooth surfaces. There are no hard and fast rules about using particular paints for particular projects, but they each have different qualities and some are more suitable for certain techniques. I always look for durability as well as a professional finish. What could be more disappointing than to complete a project only to discover a few weeks later that the paint has begun to chip, or wash off. Ceramic items that come into contact with food need to be particularly durable, so I use the waterbased porcelain paints that are baked in the oven. Ornamental items however, can be decorated using any of the paints. Glass pieces cry out for translucent glass paints and metal items for a more opaque coverage. As you become familiar with the paints, the decision as to which type to use will become more obvious.

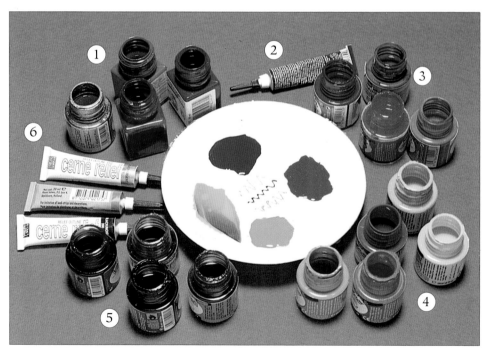

1. *Non-waterbased ceramic paints*
2. *Waterbased porcelain paint outliners*
3. *Waterbased porcelain paints*
4. *Waterbased acrylic paints*
5. *Non-waterbased glass paints*
6. *Glass painting outliners*

Waterbased porcelain paints

These paints are available in transparent, semi-transparent and opaque ranges and in a variety of colours which are intermixable. Decorated items must be baked in a domestic oven to make them durable. The paints can be applied thinly to reveal brushstrokes, or thickly for a more opaque finish. They are touch dry within half an hour, which is a great advantage when painting a multi-coloured piece. A smaller range of colours and metallic finishes are available in outliner form. These are squeezed from a tube to provide a fine outline which is useful for more detailed work.

Painted pieces should be left to air-dry for twenty-four hours, or longer if the paint has been applied thickly. Baking hardens the glaze and produces a highly professional finish. Set the temperature of the oven to 150–160°C (300–325°F or gas mark 2–3). Place your item in the cold oven and then allow it to slowly heat up – this prevents fragile pieces from cracking. When the oven reaches the required temperature, bake for thirty-five minutes. It is a good idea to bake a test piece first on an old tile as oven temperatures vary slightly.

Waterbased acrylic paints

These air-drying paints are available in a large range of colours and in a gloss, matt or pearl finish. They produce an excellent flat finish (see the terracotta pots on pages 280–285) and dry quickly between coats. If used on metal or ceramicware the finished piece should be given a coat of clear varnish for added protection. Items can be cleaned in warm soapy water and polished dry.

These flowers are outlined using black outliner and then filled in with waterbased porcelain paints.

Waterbased porcelain paints are applied using large, random brush strokes.

Waterbased acrylic paints are used to paint flowers on to a yellow base. They are then outlined with a brush and randomly sponged.

Non-waterbased ceramic paints

These air-drying paints are available in a good range of colours. They are intermixable and are excellent for opaque coverage. Brushes should be cleaned in white spirit. Beautiful dribbling and splattering effects can be created using these paints (see pages 245 and 296–300). Outliners are not available in this range, but for finer detailing, paint can be decanted into a small plastic bottle fitted with a 0.5mm metal nozzle. The paint can then be piped on to the surface. The drying time for these paints is considerably longer than for waterbased paints. Paints are touch dry within four hours and completely dry in twenty-four hours. The durability of this paint is good, but added protection can be given with a coat of clear varnish. Clean your finished piece by washing in warm soapy water, then polish dry.

Non-waterbased ceramic paint is sponged on to the surface and whilst still wet it is oversponged with white spirit which is allowed to dribble.

Random brush strokes are applied using a 1cm (½in) decorative wash brush and non-waterbased ceramic paint.

Spirals of black and gold are applied using non-waterbased ceramic paint. When dry, freestyle decorative flowers are added.

Non-waterbased glass paints

These air-drying transparent paints are available in a good range of colours and are intermixable. Clear gloss glass painting varnish can be added to the paints to dilute the colours and create a more pastel range. Brushes should be cleaned in white spirit. Tubes of outliner are available in black, imitation lead, gold, silver and copper. You can use these paints for the dribbling technique (see pages 296–297). Paints are touch dry within two hours and completely dry in eight hours. You can protect your finished pieces with a coat of clear gloss glass painting varnish. Clean your finished piece by washing in cold water, then polish dry. Items painted with glass paints are purely decorative and are not suitable for everyday use.

Blue and green non-waterbased glass paints are sponged on to the vase and allowed to dry. The surface is then decorated with glass droplets, and embellished with sun rays and swirls using the imitation lead outliner.

The design is drawn on with black outliner. When dry, it is filled in using non-waterbased glass paints diluted with clear gloss glass painting varnish to create a pastel finish.

The spiral is outlined, painted with non-waterbased glass paints, then decorated with glass droplets and metallic outliners. The remaining areas are sponged and embellished with outlined gold stars.

Other equipment and materials

You do not need all the items featured here to begin decorative painting. A list of the equipment and materials required accompanies each project, so check this carefully before you begin.

1. **Blanks** Plain ceramic, glass and enamel pieces are readily available.

2. **Lighter fuel** This can be used to remove glue, labels and traces of grease from items before decorating. Methylated spirit may also be used.

3. **White spirit** This is used for cleaning brushes used with non-waterbased paints. It is also sponged over wet non-waterbased paints for the dribbling and splattering technique (see pages 245, 296–297).

4. **Varnish** Items painted with waterbased acrylic paints, non-waterbased ceramic paints and glass paints can be given a coat of clear varnish to protect the surface decoration.

5. **Palette** You can use a plastic palette, but a white ceramic plate covered with plastic wrap provides a cheap alternative. Simply throw away the wrap when you have finished painting.

6. **Masking tape** This is used for masking off areas that you want to remain unpainted.

7. **Pieces of sponge** Sponge can be used to apply paint. Buy a large, inexpensive one and tear off small pieces as needed.

8. **Cooling rack** This is used for drying finished painted items on.

9. **Cotton buds** Mistakes and dribbles can be removed with these.

10. **Scissors** Graphite, carbon and tracing papers can be cut to size with scissors.

11. **String** This is used to measure the rim of a pot and to help position designs (see page 282).

12. **Brushes** The projects use Nos. 2, 4 and 6 paintbrushes, a 1cm (½in) flat brush and a No. 6 rigger brush. Always look after your brushes carefully – they are the tools of your trade and should be cherished. Wash them in water or white spirit, depending on the type of paint used.

13. **Pencils** You can draw directly on to surfaces with a soft pencil (4B). A hard pencil (H) can be used when tracing a design with carbon or graphite paper.

14. **Ballpoint pen** This can be used instead of a hard pencil to transfer a design when using carbon or graphite paper.

15. **Fine waterbased felt-tip pen** Designs can be drawn directly on to the surface using this.

16. **Scalpel** Use a sharp scalpel or craft knife to cut out a stencil from stencil paper (see page 297).

17. **Cocktail sticks** These are used to scratch away areas of paint (see page 254).

18. **Tracing paper** This is used to trace your designs from the patterns in the book.

19. **Carbon paper** A transfer paper which will produce a definite and durable line to work to. It is useful when transferring designs on to glass if outliner is to cover the carbon line.

20. **Graphite paper** This is a transfer paper which will produce a soft guideline to work to. It is particularly useful when painting a pale-coloured object, as this softer line will not show through the paint.

21. **Stamps** Foam stamps mounted on to wood or clear plastic blocks are ideal for stamping on to smooth surfaces. Clear plastic blocks make it easier to position the stamp correctly.

22. **Stencil paper** This is available in different thicknesses. The finer the gauge of paper, the easier it is to cut. Acetate can also be used.

23. **Fine sandpaper** Metal items will require sanding before painting to remove any rust or uneven spots.

24. **Absorbent paper** This is an absolute necessity and is used for mopping up spillages or wiping away mistakes.

Using colour

The paints used in this book are available in a huge range of colours. However, by using just the primary colours– red, blue and yellow – you can produce a good basic range. The colour wheels on these pages provide you with a guide to refer to when deciding on your own colour combinations. The primary colours on each wheel are indicated by the small dots within the inner wheel.

Waterbased porcelain paints

These paints are baked in a domestic oven to make them more durable. The outer wheel shows how a flat vibrant range can be produced if the paints are applied generously. The inner wheel shows that, when applied thinly, brushstrokes are revealed and a more pastel range is obtained; this use of the paint is particularly effective for the one-stroke flowers and leaves (see pages 242 and 274–275).

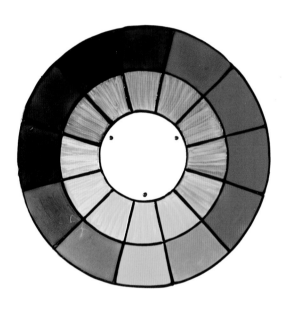

When baking the paints, timing and temperature are extremely important (see page 233). Underbaking will reduce the durability; overbaking will dull the colours.

USING WATERBASED OUTLINERS

The outliners provided in this range can be used in conjunction with the paint or on their own as shown here. The metallic outliners are particularly effective when piped over a prepainted surface as fine detailing (see page 65).

Non-waterbased ceramic paints

These paints are air-dried rather than baked in a domestic oven. The outer wheel shows the range of colours that can be produced by mixing the three primary colours. The inner wheel shows the pastel range that can be achieved by adding white paint.

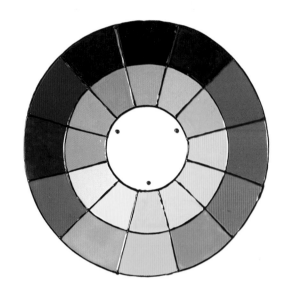

Non-waterbased glass paints

Glass paints are air-drying and have to be applied generously to obtain a flat, stained-glass effect. Sometimes, the paints may appear a little dense. The outer wheel shows the paint applied straight from the bottle, the inner wheel shows the colours achieved by adding clear gloss glass painting varnish; this lightens the density of the paint without reducing the viscosity. If you dilute the paints with white spirit, they will become thinner and brushstrokes will become visible.

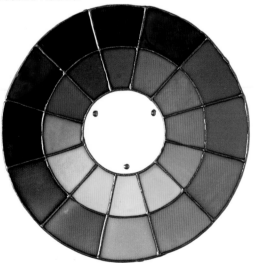

USING NON-WATERBASED OUTLINERS

There are no outliners in the non-waterbased ceramic paint range, so if you want to outline, you can decant the paint into a small plastic bottle fitted with a 0.5mm metal nozzle. Alternatively, use glass painting outliners. Black and imitation lead glass painting outliners are used to outline the basic design. It is best to apply the metallic outliners as decoration on top of a finished painted piece (see page 266), as the paints colour the lines. Outliners are ideal for lettering projects and can also be used to decorate wood, papier mâché and card.

Surfaces

These before and after photographs show clearly how plain pieces can be beautifully transformed using the right paints and a little imagination. All the techniques shown opposite are covered in the projects in this book. The techniques are simple, but it is important to prepare surfaces correctly before you start to paint. Items should be completely grease-free in order for the paint to adhere to a smooth surface.

Use a soft cloth and lighter fuel or methylated spirit to wipe over glass and ceramicware. Old metalware should be rubbed down with fine sandpaper to remove any rust spots or irregularities, then wiped down as described above to remove all debris and traces of grease. New metalware should be sanded down lightly and then wiped down. Terracotta pots should be scrubbed clean in soapy water, then dried thoroughly before decorating.

Terracotta pots, glass bottles and bowls, ceramic vases, tiles and cups, and metal goblets and bottles can all be decorated with the paints shown in this book. Here, the items have been stencilled, freepainted, finely detailed, dribbled, outlined, sponged and embellished with beads. The techniques are simple – all you need are the paints, the materials and a little imagination.

The blank items opposite were found in kitchen shops, DIY shops, garden centres and junk shops. The same items are shown above, fully decorated.

Decorative effects

Many of the techniques described in this section are used in the projects. There is no limit to the wonderful finishes you can achieve with a few paints and some simple tools. Do not be frightened to experiment. Sponging, stamping, dribbling and masking all are great fun and you will certainly create some interesting effects.

Waterbased porcelain paints

All the effects shown on these two pages have been created using waterbased porcelain paints that have been baked in an oven. It is possible to create similar effects using waterbased acrylic paints or non-waterbased ceramic or glass paints.

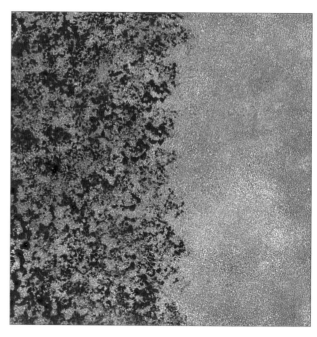

Sponging   *The background is sponged with a fine sponge using light blue paint. Darker blue is worked over the base coat using a coarser sponge to create texture.*

Using random brushstrokes   *Transparent blue paint is applied randomly and quickly to the base using a 1cm (½in) flat paintbrush. When dry, transparent yellow paint is applied on top.*

Freestyle one-stroke painting   *The flower petals and leaves are painted in one at a time using blue and green transparent paint. The stems are added with one stroke of a rigger brush.*

Outlining *The designs shown at the top are outlined using coloured outliners, and the bird panel below is created using copper paint decanted into a plastic bottle fitted with a 0.5mm metal nozzle.*

Stencilling *The background is sponged with opaque violet. When dry, the butterfly stencil design is sponged on using a selection of darker colours.*

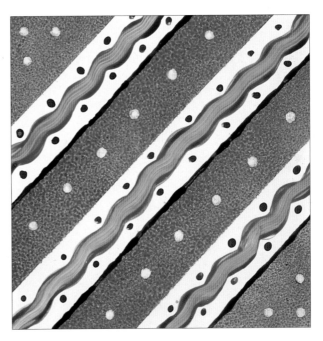

Stamping *A double row of small squares is stamped around the border using blue paint and a small square stamp. The centre is stamped with a blue daisy. The orange detailing is painted on.*

Masking *Strips of masking tape are applied then the unmasked areas are sponged blue. White dots are wiped out with a cotton bud whilst the paint is still wet. The masking tape is removed and the purple lines and dots are added with a paintbrush.*

Non-waterbased paints

The effects shown on these two pages are created using non-waterbased glass and ceramic paints. You can clearly see the difference between the transparent glass paints and the more opaque ceramic paints.

On this page, glass surfaces are used to demonstrate the techniques of sponging, outlining and embellishing using metallic outliners and glass beads. The designs on the page opposite are worked on a white ceramic base and introduce you to dribbling and splattering techniques. These opaque paints are ideal for folk art where vibrant flat colours are required (see pages 271 and 294).

Mottled sponging   *This glass surface is sponged using two contrasting colours and a fine sponge.*

Embellishing   *The surface is randomly sponged with blue and green. When dry, the heart is outlined and filled in with metallic outliner. The central glass droplet is pressed into the outliner whilst it is still wet, and small beads are embedded around the edge.*

Outlining and painting   *The design is laid under the glass and is then outlined with black outliner. When dry, it is painted. Finally metallic outliners are used to add more detail.*

244

Creating an opaque finish *A large flat brush is used to apply a generous coat of paint. The brushstrokes are applied in the same direction to achieve a flat finish.*

Blending colours *Bands of darker and lighter blues are overlapped using a large flat brush. They are then blended together.*

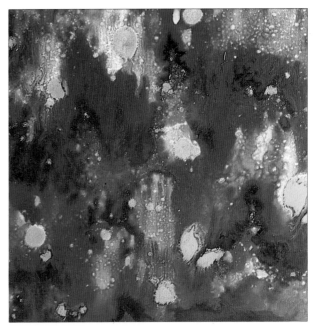

Dribbling *The background is randomly sponged with blues and greens. Whilst still wet, it is lightly oversponged with white spirit and tilted so that the paints run down the surface.*

Splattering *The background is randomly sponged with turquoise and dark blue. Whilst still wet, it is oversponged with white spirit. A toothbrush is used to flick and splatter gold paint on to the surface.*

Tulip mug

SPONGING, STAMPING AND PAINTING

Sponging and stamping are the quickest and easiest ways of decorating china, yet the results are very professional. With a stamp, a few paints and some sponge, you can transform a plain mug into something special. Who knows, after completing this project, perhaps you will be inspired to stamp a complete set of mugs for your family.

YOU WILL NEED
White ceramic mug
Waterbased porcelain paints: dark green, light green, scarlet and yellow
3 pieces of coarse sponge
Masking tape
Tulip flower stamp
Stem and leaf stamp
1cm (½in) flat brush
No. 6 paintbrush
Palette

1. Mask the base of the handle with masking tape. Transfer your paints to the palette. Form a piece of sponge into a pad, tucking in all hard edges. Sponge the bottom third of the mug with dark green paint. Allow to dry.

2. Use a clean piece of sponge to oversponge the dark green with light green. Go over the edge slightly so that the light green shows above the dark green band. Allow to dry.

3. Paint the stem and leaf stamp with dark green paint using a No. 6 paintbrush.

4. Stamp stems and leaves evenly around the mug so that the bottom of each stem rests on the light green sponging. Allow to dry.

246

5. Paint the tulip flower stamp with scarlet. Stamp a tulip flower at the top of each stem. Allow to dry. Overstamp each flower with scarlet to strengthen the colour. Allow to dry.

6. Use a clean piece of sponge and yellow paint to sponge the rim of the mug and the areas in between the flowers. Allow to dry.

7. Remove the masking tape from the handle. Use a 1cm (½in) flat brush to paint the handle yellow. Leave to dry for twenty-four hours before baking (see page 233).

The finished mug

This cheerful mug is easy to paint, and a matching mini teapot can be decorated in the same way. Here, I have painted the spout yellow and sponged the lid green.

247

Floral cup and saucer

These are sponged all over with yellow then the roses and leaves are painted in. The design is loosely outlined in black. Swirls are added to the centre of each flower. The areas between the flowers, the handle and edges are sponged in red.

Blue and white spotted mug

The rim of the mug is masked with masking tape and circular stickers are randomly applied around the mug. It is then sponged first with mid-blue, then with dark blue. Finally, the stickers and masking tape are removed.

Multicoloured striped and spotted mug

The mug is loosely painted with stripes of different colours. Dots and squiggles are then added.

Red and blue mottled cup

The cup is sponged using red and blue paints. When dry it is decorated with squiggles and dots using gold outliner.

Blue and white floral mug

This white mug is decorated with freestyle one-stroke painting.

Striped enamel mug

A 1cm (½in) flat brush is used to create wavy lines of different colours.

Cherry enamel mug

The lower edge of this mug is stamped with small red squares. The cherries are stamped around the middle, then the leaves and stems are painted in.

Waterbased porcelain paints are used on all these cups and mugs. Once baked, the paint is durable and items can be washed frequently.

Cat mug

Waterbased porcelain paints are used to create this mug. The cat design is transferred on to the front of the mug using carbon paper and the pattern provided. The design is outlined in black and allowed to dry. Masking tape is applied to the rim, the design is then filled in with paint and allowed to dry. The background is painted blue using random brushstrokes. The masking tape is removed and the rim and handle are painted yellow.

Pattern for the cat mug

Biscuit barrel

This cheerful biscuit barrel is decorated using the masking, sponging and stamping techniques. Durable waterbased porcelain paints are used as this item will need to be washed frequently. Three evenly spaced bands of masking tape are wrapped around the barrel and strips of tape are criss-crossed over the lid. The barrel and lid are sponged with bright colours and the masking tape is then removed. When dry, the uncoloured areas are sponged yellow. The barrel and lid are then stamped with a small heart-shaped stamp to complete the decoration. The lid knob is painted in a coordinating colour.

Grape tile

TRANSFERRING A DESIGN, MASKING, BRUSHWORK, OUTLINING AND HIGHLIGHTING

The techniques used in this project will give you a good opportunity to try out the paints and outliner. The grapes are coloured using the paint sparingly so that the texture of the brushstrokes is revealed. In contrast, plenty of paint is used to give a flat finish to the leaves and outer border. I have used a 15cm (6in) tile, but you can use any sized tile, and adjust the size of the pattern accordingly.

Students often ask me how to decorate tiles that are already glued into place on a wall and the answer is that it is not easy! If possible, tiles should be decorated flat before gluing into position. Certainly, for this project that is essential. However, if this is not possible, try masking around the tile to be decorated and then sponging paint on to form a base colour. The stamping or stencilling techniques shown elsewhere in this book are ideal for decorating vertical surfaces, as very little paint is applied and therefore runs are not a problem.

YOU WILL NEED
White ceramic tile
Waterbased porcelain paints: cream, blue, purple and green
Waterbased black outliner
Paintbrushes, Nos. 6 and 2
Piece of fine sponge
Cocktail stick
Masking tape
Tracing paper
Scissors
Fine black felt-tip pen
Ballpoint pen
Graphite paper
Palette

Pattern for the grape tile

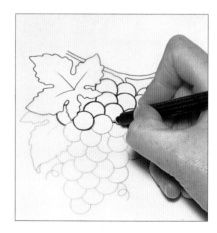

1. Trace the pattern provided using a fine black felt-tip pen, or photocopy it directly on to a piece of paper if you prefer.

2. Cut the tracing paper approximately 0.5cm (¼in) smaller than the tile. Cut out a piece of graphite paper the same size as the tracing paper. Tape the top of the tracing paper to the tile; slip the graphite paper face down under the tracing paper and then tape the bottom to secure.

3. Trace over the outlined pattern with a ballpoint pen. Press firmly so that the design is transferred clearly on to the tile. Remove the tracing and graphite paper.

4. Use the black outliner to carefully outline the design. Work from the top of the tile, and gently squeeze the tube with an even pressure to produce a smooth, unbroken line. Do not outline the tendrils as these will be painted in at a later stage.

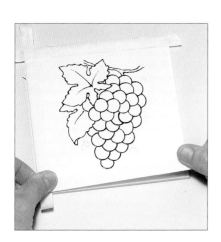

5. Mask around the edges and corners of the tile with masking tape. Press the edges of the tape down firmly, so that paint will not seep underneath.

6. Pour a little cream paint on to a palette. Sponge in a border around the outlined design. Remove the masking tape immediately, and allow to dry.

7. Paint in the grapes using blue paint and a No. 6 paintbrush. Try to get the brushstrokes working with the shape of the grapes. Do not leave to dry.

8. Dip a cocktail stick in water then use this to wipe out a dot of blue paint from the top right-hand corner of each grape to create highlights. Leave to dry.

9. Lightly shade the base of each grape using a little purple paint and a No. 6 brush. Allow to dry.

10. Paint the leaves and stem green using a No. 6 brush. Apply the paint generously when painting the leaves and try to avoid brushmarks.

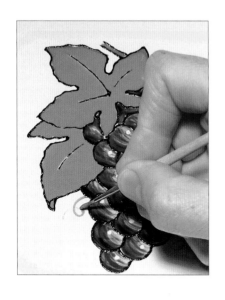

11. Paint the small tendrils in green using a No. 2 brush.

12. Use a No. 6 paintbrush and purple paint to fill in the outer border. Apply the paint generously to avoid brush-strokes. Turn the tile around as you work. Allow to dry for twenty-four hours before baking (see page 233).

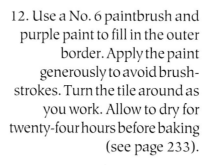

The finished tile

One or two of these vibrant tiles placed around your kitchen will add a touch of class to a plain wall. Alternatively, the finished tile could be framed, or used as a teapot stand.

Variation

You can paint your tile to match your own decor. Just by deepening the colour of the grapes and adding a dark blue border and an extra leaf, this tile looks quite different.

255

Use your imagination to create unusual tiles to decorate your home. Patterns for the designs can be found on pages 34–39).

Red apple tile

The apples and leaves are outlined in black then painted red and green. The highlights on the apples are wiped out with a cotton bud, and a blue background is painted in.

Colourful cat tile

The design is outlined using metallic copper outliner and filled in with bright, vibrant colours.

Fleur de lys tile

The blue background is sponged on, then the fleur de lys motif is stencilled in gold.

Sun tile

The design is outlined in blue using a paintbrush. The yellow areas are painted in and the red detail is added. Red and yellow are then sponged around the border.

Cat and mouse tile

The design is outlined in red outliner, then green and pink paint are sponged on to the cat. Blue paint is sponged on to the mice and the border is sponged in blue.

Fish tile

The fish is outlined in blue using simple strokes. Details are added and the fish is painted yellow. When dry, a thin wash of green paint is applied to the background.

Fruit tile

The design is outlined in black and filled in with strong Mediterranean colours.

Mermaid tile

The design is outlined with black outliner on to a mirror tile and painted with diluted glass paints.

Rose tile

The background is sponged yellow then the roses and leaves are painted in. The design is loosely outlined in black, using a brush. Swirls are added to the centre of each flower.

Pattern for the colourful cat tile featured on pages 256–257

Pattern for the fruit tile featured on pages 257–257

Pattern for the red apple tile featured on pages 256–257

Pattern for the mermaid tile featured on pages 256–257

*Pattern for the cat and mouse tile
featured on pages 256–257*

*Pattern for the fish tile featured
on pages 256–257*

Pattern for the rose tile featured on pages 256–257

Pattern for the sun tile featured on pages 256–257

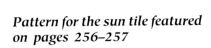

Festive plate

OUTLINING AND PAINTING

I love Christmas, and what better way to decorate your home than with this colourful festive plate. Placed on a windowsill or lit from behind with a candle on a mantelpiece, you will be able to see clearly the wonderful vibrancy of the stained-glass colours. Remember to apply the paint generously to avoid brushmarks.

You can use a plate of any size for this project – simply adjust the pattern on a photocopier to fit. The outliner will take approximately half an hour to harden, so work carefully to avoid smudging. Mistakes can be removed with a cotton bud if the outliner is still wet; alternatively you can let it harden then carefully scrape it off with a knife.

YOU WILL NEED

Glass plate

Non-waterbased glass paints: red, yellow, orange, green and blue

Clear gloss glass painting varnish

Black and gold glass painting outliners

Masking tape

Soft paintbrush, No. 4

Palette

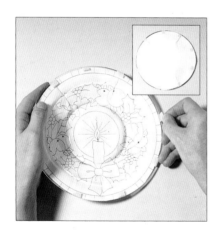

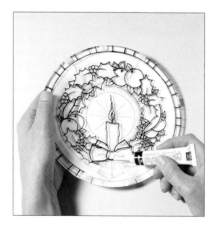

1. Photocopy the pattern opposite on to paper then cut it out. Place the design on the underside of the plate, then pleat the paper so that it lies flat against the glass. Tape into position with small pieces of masking tape. Do not put masking tape over any of the black lines of the pattern.

2. Outline the design (excluding the dots around the candle) using the black outliner. Gently squeeze the tube to produce a smooth, even line. Work from the top of the plate down, being careful not to smudge the outliner. Leave it to harden.

3. Use gold outliner to apply a circle of dots around the central candle flame. Allow to dry, then remove the pattern but do not throw it away. The remaining gold decoration will be added after the painting has been completed.

Pattern for the festive plate

4. Mix one part yellow paint with four parts clear varnish and use this to paint the candle. Use a No. 4 paintbrush and apply the paint mixture generously to avoid brushmarks. Paint the centre of the flame red and the outer part orange. Paint yellow around the candle, up to the circle of gold dots.

5. Paint the berries, the ribbon and the bow with red. Carefully fill in the oranges using yellow. While the yellow paint is still wet, blend a little red and orange around the bottom of each orange to create shading.

6. Paint the holly leaves green. Mix a few drops of green with yellow and then use this olive colour to paint the leaves of the oranges.

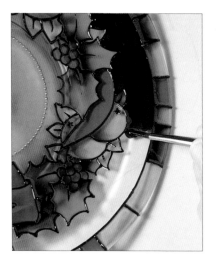

7. Paint the outer rim sections in alternating colours. Use all the colours on your palette. Allow to dry overnight.

8. Use orange paint to fill in the background area surrounding the central yellow circle. Paint the remaining border blue. Allow to dry overnight.

9. Place the pattern underneath the plate. Follow the design and use gold outliner to add dots around the flame. Finally, decorate with gold stars. Leave to dry for twenty-four hours.

The finished plate

*This is a favourite design of mine, and it often inspires people to take up
glass painting as a hobby!*

Butterfly bowl

This octagonal glass bowl is decorated with non-waterbased glass paints and black outliner. A butterfly is transferred on to each side of the bowl using the pattern provided and carbon paper. The first butterfly is outlined and a line of outliner is piped around it. This is allowed to dry before moving on to the next butterfly. The bowl is worked in this way until all the sides are outlined. A row of vertical lines are added around the rim border and allowed to dry. One butterfly and background area is painted and left to dry before moving on to the next. This means that you are always working on a flat surface and the paints can dry flat. Finally, the rim border sections are decorated with different colours and, when dry, the base is painted.

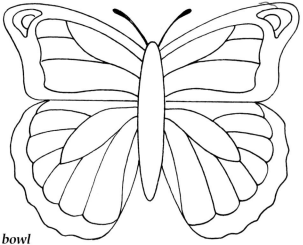

Pattern for the butterfly bowl

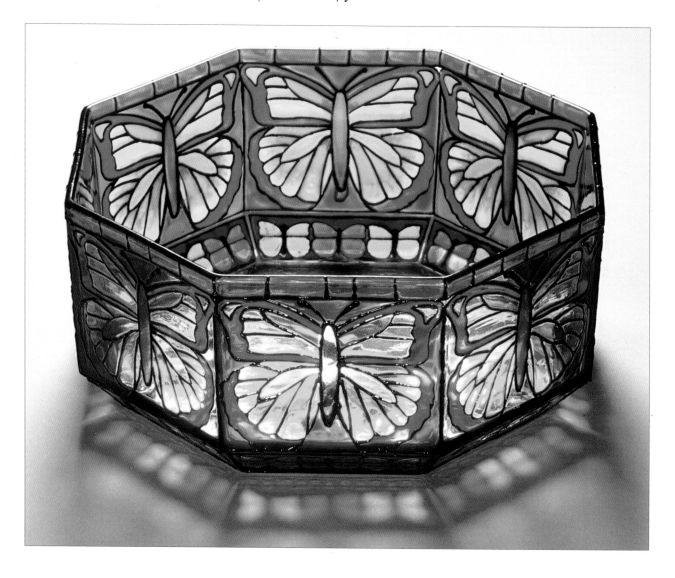

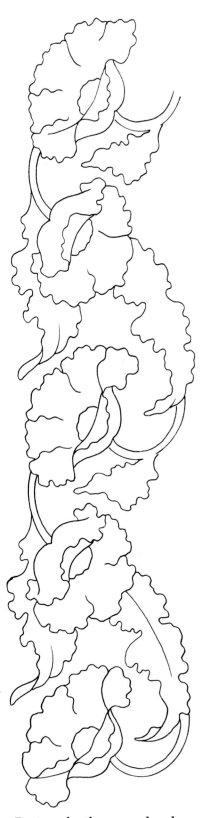

Pattern for the poppy bowl

Poppy bowl

This glass poppy bowl is outlined and painted on the outside using transparent waterbased porcelain paints. It is then sponged on the inside using metallic waterbased porcelain paints. The size of the pattern is increased so that it fits around the inside of the bowl. It is taped into position so that the design shows through the bowl. The design is outlined in black on the outside and allowed to dry. The poppy flowers, leaves and stems are then painted in. When dry, the inside of the bowl is sponged with copper paint.

Pink, pale blue and gold plate

Non-waterbased pink and gold ceramic paints are used to sponge the plate. The fine floral tracery is piped on using gold paint decanted into a plastic bottle fitted with a 0.5mm metal nozzle.

Eastern plate

Waterbased porcelain paints and outliners are used to create this plate. The design is transferred on to the plate using carbon paper and the pattern provided on page 273. It is then outlined with black outliner. The sections are painted in, working from the centre outwards. Gold outliner is used to add detail.

Stripy sunshine plate

The rim of this plate is decorated with stripes of bold colour using waterbased porcelain paints. When dry, dots and squiggles are added in contrasting colours and the centre is painted, leaving brushstrokes visible.

Embellished plate

The rim of this plate is masked before the centre is sponged with non-waterbased ceramic paints. While still wet, it is lightly oversponged with white spirit. The masking tape is removed and the plate allowed to dry before sponging the rim. When the rim is dry, glass droplets are glued into place then outlined in imitation lead outliner.

Mediterranean plate

Waterbased porcelain paints are used on this plate. The rim is painted loosely with fruits and leaves, then the centre is painted in a coordinating colour.

Folk art plate

This enamel plate is painted using non-waterbased ceramic paints to give a smooth flat finish. It is given two coats of the base colour. The design is drawn on to the plate using a white chinagraph pencil following the pattern provided on page 272. The flower petals and leaves are painted in bold colours using the one-stroke technique (see pages 274–275).

271

*Patterns for the folk art
plate featured on page 271*

Patterns for the Eastern plate featured on page 271

Floral vase

FREEPAINTING

The loosely painted flowers and leaves in this project do not require great artistry, yet the overall effect is professional. This is a freepainting project. The pattern is provided as a guide to be used when painting the flowers and leaves. The arrows show the direction of the brushstrokes. Each flower, petal, stem and leaf is created with one stroke of the brush. The petals are pulled towards the centre of the flower, and the leaves are pulled towards the stem. Practice this one-stroke painting on paper before working on your vase so that you become familiar with the technique.

YOU WILL NEED

White ceramic vase
Waterbased porcelain paints:
pale pink, dark pink,
blue and gold
3 pieces of sponge
Paintbrushes, Nos. 4 and 6
Rigger paintbrush, No. 6
Palette

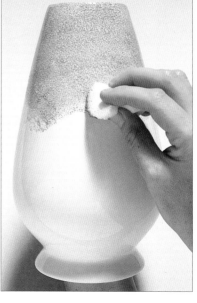

1. Sponge the entire vase with pale pink paint. Work as evenly as possible. Leave to dry.

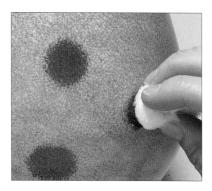

2. Randomly sponge assorted sized blue spots over the surface of the vase to form the flower heads. Allow to dry.

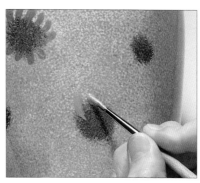

3. Use a No. 4 paintbrush and gold paint for the flower petals. Paint the top row first. Turn the vase and paint the bottom row of smaller petals. Leave to dry.

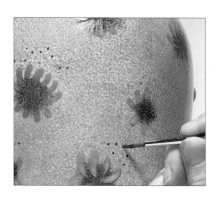

4. Add dots of gold and blue around each flower to represent pollen grains.

5. Paint in the stems using dark pink and a No. 6 rigger paintbrush.

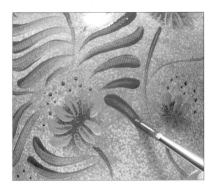

6. Use a No. 6 paintbrush and dark pink to paint the leaves. Fill in spaces with leaves to cover the whole vase.

7. Sponge the rim gold. Leave to dry for twenty-four hours before baking (see page 233).

The finished vase

This vase is painted using the one-stroke technique. You can vary the colour combinations to produce different effects (see pages 241 and 277).

LEFT

Daisy vase

This glass vase is painted all over using non-waterbased glass paints, then it is left to dry. The daisy design is drawn on using a white chinagraph pencil. Non-waterbased ceramic paints are used to paint the leaves, flowers and pollen grains.

OPPOSITE

All these vases are painted using waterbased porcelain paints.

Floral vase

This vase is decorated using the basic one-stroke technique described on pages 274–275.

Relief vase

The basic colours are sponged on to the surface of this raised relief vase to give a mottled effect. When dry, gold highlights are sponged along the edges of the flower petals.

Abstract vase

This is probably one of the simplest pieces in the book. The vase is painted with random brushstrokes of alternating colour using a 1cm (½in) brush. The rim is then sponged with a coordinating colour.

Afternoon tea set

The items on this page are decorated using opaque waterbased porcelain paints and the freepainting one-stroke technique (see pages 274–275). Odd pieces can be painted with the same design to produce a matching set. The base coat is sponged on and allowed to dry before adding the one-stroke flowers and leaves. Rims and edges are sponged with gold.

OPPOSITE

Traditional coffee set

This coffee set is decorated using opaque waterbased porcelain paints. It is an extension of the freepainting one-stroke technique described on pages 274–275. The pieces are first sponged with a pastel colour and allowed to dry. They are then randomly sponged with small spots of paint to form a background for the floral decorations. The white flowers are painted in with a brush and the flower centres added. The leaves are painted using the one-stroke technique. When dry, the edges and rims are sponged with gold paint.

Flower pots

VERDIGRISING

This classic urn would grace any patio. The subtle verdigris finish and gold sponging highlight the relief pattern found on this terracotta pot. It is in fact a very easy technique to create with a few paints and pieces of sponge.

YOU WILL NEED

Terracotta pot
Waterbased acrylic paints: black, dark green, emerald green, light green and gold
3 pieces of sponge
No. 6 paintbrush
Palette

The finished urn

Keep an eye open for pots with unusual shapes – new or old, they can easily be cleaned up and transformed with a few paints and this simple verdigrising technique.

1. Use black paint and a No. 6 paintbrush to paint around the raised design and into the crevices.

2. Mix dark and emerald green paint with a little water, then sponge this all over the pot. Rub the paint into the crevices, allowing the black to show through slightly. Leave to dry.

3. Sponge light green paint on to the raised areas, and those which would weather naturally. The pot should now be completely covered in paint.

4. Use a sponge to dab a little gold paint over the light green areas, then rub it in to leave a subtle golden sheen.

MASKING, SPONGING AND STAMPING

This is a quick but very effective project. The simplicity of the white daisy stamped against a vivid blue background has transformed this ordinary plant pot. Sponging the rim is easier and quicker than painting it, and this creates a soft edge to the pot.

YOU WILL NEED

Terracotta pot
Waterbased acrylic paints:
bright blue, white and orange
Masking tape
Paintbrush, No. 4
1cm (½in) flat brush
Daisy stamp
Sponge
Palette

1. Mask the top of the pot with masking tape. Press the edges of the masking tape down firmly. Do not mask the rim.

2. Sponge the rim with blue paint. Paint the main section of the pot using a 1cm (½in) flat brush. Remove the masking tape. Leave to dry.

3. Apply white paint to the daisy stamp. Stamp a daisy in the centre of the main blue section of the pot. Leave to dry.

4. Add lots of tiny dots of orange paint to the centre of the daisy using a No. 4 paintbrush. Leave to dry.

The finished pot
This is a cheerful design and the pot can be used either indoors or out. The waterbased acrylic paints used in this and other projects give an excellent flat coverage and provide a weather-resistant finish.

PAINTING, SPONGING AND MASKING

Red tulips add a splash of colour to any garden. With its yellow background and bold green leaves, this cheerful pot will brighten up even the dullest day.

Pattern for the tulip pot

YOU WILL NEED

Terracotta pot

Waterbased acrylic paint: red, yellow, orange, bright green and dark green

Sponge

String

1cm (½in) flat brush

Masking tape

No. 4 paintbrush

Tracing paper

Ballpoint pen

Scissors

Graphite paper

Palette

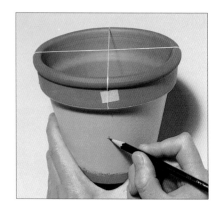

1. Mask the top of the pot with masking tape (see page 281). Sponge the rim red and paint the main section yellow. Leave to dry, then apply another coat of yellow to the main section. Allow to dry.

2. Sponge a band of bright green all the way around the base of the pot.

3. Divide the pot into quarters as shown. Mark the four points half way up the pot for the position of the tulips, using the string as a guide.

5. Trace the tulip pattern on to tracing paper. Cut it out and tape it on to the pot, positioning the middle of the tulip head over one of the four pencil marks. Slide graphite paper underneath. Trace over the outline with a ballpoint pen to transfer the design. Repeat until you have four tulips.

The finished pot

This simple design is painted on using the pattern provided, to create the tulip shapes. Try painting different flowers around your pot – sunflowers, poppies, daisies and roses can all look very effective, and you can vary your background colour to complement the design.

6. Paint in the flowers. Add orange dots between each tulip head. Allow to dry, then add stripes of shading to the tulip heads and leaves.

PAGES 284–285

Selection of terracotta pots

Group your decorated pots together to create a colourful display in your garden. Limit your colour palette for a more coordinated look. The main colours used to decorate these pots are red, yellow, blue and green. Simple spots and stripes are easy to paint but they look very effective. A border of strawberries painted around the rim of a larger pot adds a spot of colour whilst you are waiting for those early flowers to bloom. An overall design of fruit or flowers will take a little more time to do but is well worth the effort. Get out those paints and pots and have a go!

283

Perfume bottle

PAINTING AND EMBELLISHING

The addition of beads and metallic outliner to a painted glass bottle really does transform it. Use rich, vibrant colours and choose beads to match or complement the background colours. I have used turquoise and clear glass beads for this bottle, but you could use more strongly contrasting colours if you wish. Group a few decorated bottles together on a windowsill to create a stunning effect and reveal the beauty of these paints.

YOU WILL NEED

Small flat-sided glass bottle with cork
Silver glass painting outliner
Small beads
Non-waterbased glass paints: turquoise
Tracing paper
Ballpoint pen
Scissors
Carbon paper
Masking tape
Cocktail stick
Paintbrush, No. 4

Pattern for the perfume bottle

1. Trace the heart pattern on to tracing paper. Cut it out and tape it on to the bottle. Slide carbon paper underneath. Trace over the outline with a ballpoint pen to transfer the design then remove the masking tape, tracing and carbon paper.

2. Outline the heart with silver outliner. Fill in the heart with the outliner, then use the nozzle to smooth out the paste.

3. Immediately lie the bottle on a plate. Sprinkle the heart with beads, then arrange them carefully using a cocktail stick. Fill in any spaces using beads from the plate, picked up on the cocktail stick. Leave the outliner to harden.

4. Use the silver outliner to add a diamond shape to one of the four corners. Decorate with beads (see step 3). Repeat on the other three corners. Leave the outliner to harden.

5. Hold the neck of the bottle then paint the bottle turquoise, starting at the bottom. Carefully paint around the beaded sections. When you get near the top, stand the bottle up to paint the neck. Allow to dry.

6. Use the outliner to add dots in a line between each beaded diamond section and towards the neck of the bottle. Add a row of dots down each edge of the bottle. Allow to dry.

7. Paint the sides of the cork with silver outliner using a No. 4 brush. Leave to dry. Apply a thick layer of outliner directly from the tube to the top of the cork. Decorate immediately with beads. Allow to dry.

The finished bottle

Sparkling glass beads look stunning against the rich turquoise of this bottle.

PAGES 288–289

Selection of perfume bottles

Empty miniature bottles provide unusual shapes to decorate. Designs can become very intricate when working on such a small scale. Remember to paint the stoppers to match the bottles.

The bottles on page 288 are decorated with glass paints and metallic outliners. The bottles on page 289 are decorated using waterbased porcelain paints and outliners.

Eastern bottle

*This metal bottle is decorated
using waterbased porcelain paints
and outliners. The patterns are
transferred on to the surface using
carbon paper. The designs are
outlined in black outliner and left
to dry. The bottle is painted and,
when dry, detailing is added using
gold outliner. The cork is removed
before baking.*

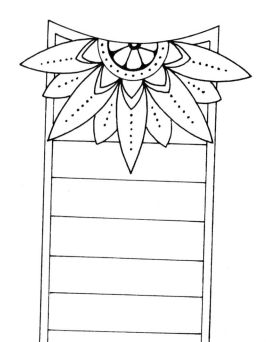

Patterns for the Eastern bottle

Biscuit tin

SPONGING, STAMPING, FREEPAINTING AND WIPING OUT

This biscuit tin started life as a coffee container. I am an inveterate hoarder and cannot bear to throw anything away. I love the feeling of satisfaction when creating something from nothing. The sponging, stamping and freepainting techniques are all combined in this project. The tin illustrated here is 20cm (8in) tall and 15cm (6in) in diameter, but you can adapt the design to fit any sized tin.

The finished tin
Simple techniques are used to create this colourful container. You can vary the colour scheme to match the decor of your own home.

YOU WILL NEED

Metal tin

Waterbased porcelain paints: white, deep blue, scarlet and olive green

Piece of fine sponge

Fine grade sandpaper

Lighter fuel or methylated spirit

Soft cloth

Cotton bud

Paintbrush, No. 6

Rigger brush, No. 6

Small circular stamp and small square stamp

Palette

1. Sand the tin to remove any rough spots or irregularities. Wipe down the tin with a soft cloth and lighter fuel or methylated spirit.

2. Sponge the tin using a fine sponge and white paint. Allow to dry thoroughly then repeat to create a good opaque base on which to work. Allow to dry.

3. Stamp on two rows of blue squares (see page 243) at the top and bottom of the tin to create a gingham border.

4. Stamp a red cherry on to the tin. Overstamp it, then use a damp cotton bud to remove a small area of paint and create a highlight. Repeat until the tin is covered in highlighted cherries. Allow to dry.

5. Use green paint and a No. 6 rigger brush to paint in the stems. Use green paint and a No. 6 paintbrush for the leaves. Add as many leaves as you like, to fill in any spaces. Leave to dry for twenty-four hours before baking (see page 233.)

Watering can

Non-waterbased ceramic paints are used on this project. The body of the can is painted blue and, when dry, it is decorated with simple one-stroke flowers in alternate colours. A striped spout and handle add the finishing touch to this zany container.

Green folk art tin

The base colour and red band around the rim are painted using non-waterbased ceramic paints. When dry, the folk art design is drawn on using a white chinagraph pencil. The flowers and leaves are painted in using the one-stroke technique (see pages 274–275).

Small lilac floral tin

This can is sponged with waterbased porcelain paints and left to dry. Simple white daisies are painted and small dots of colour are added in between the flowers.

Daisy bucket

This bucket is painted using green non-waterbased ceramic paint. When completely dry, strips of masking tape are used to create the blue and white vertical stripes and the blue line around the base. White daisies are stamped around the bottom section of the bucket and the centre of each daisy and the handle of the bucket are painted orange.

Shell bowl

DRIBBLING AND STENCILLING

This project introduces you to the dribbling technique, which can be used with all non-waterbased ceramic and glass paints. It makes an interesting decorative finish on its own, or it can be used as a background for stencilling or stamping, for example. You should use a clean piece of sponge for each colour you apply; this will maintain the vibrancy of the paints. This shell bowl is great fun to decorate, but the dribbling technique can be surprisingly messy, so protect your clothes and cover your work surface with layers of newspaper.

YOU WILL NEED

Ceramic bowl

Non-waterbased ceramic paints: royal blue, petrol blue, turquoise, deep pink and gold

6 pieces of sponge

White spirit

Stencil paper

Pencil

Saucer

Masking tape

Thick card

Scalpel or craft knife

Absorbent paper

Small tin, slightly smaller than the base of the bowl

Newspaper

Palette

The finished bowl

Striking marine colours contrast brilliantly with this gold shell motif. Filled with fragrant soaps, this bowl would enhance any bathroom.

Pattern for the shell bowl stencil

1. Pour a small pool of each colour (excluding gold) on to your palette. Sponge the entire bowl with random spots of paint using a clean piece of sponge for each colour.

2. Place the wet bowl on top of a small tin to raise it from your work surface. Pour some white spirit into a saucer, then use this to lightly sponge the surface of the bowl. Start at the rim and work down, allowing the white spirit to run.

3. Leave the bowl in position on the tin. Wipe the base with absorbent paper to remove any drips of paint. Leave to dry for twenty-four hours.

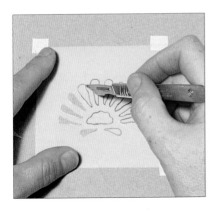

4. Trace the shell pattern opposite on to stencil paper. Tape the stencil paper on to a piece of thick card, then cut out the sections of the design using a scalpel or craft knife. Remove the masking tape.

5. Attach the stencil to the top of the bowl using masking tape. Lightly sponge over it with gold paint. Repeat, continuing the design all around the top of the bowl. Leave to dry.

6. Sponge the rim with gold paint. Leave to dry.

Fleur de lys bowl

Non-waterbased glass paints are used to sponge this glass bowl using the technique described on pages 296–297. Gold non-waterbased ceramic paints are used to stencil four fleur de lys motifs around the bowl (see the pattern on page 301). Tulip heads are stamped upside down between the motifs and the rim is then sponged gold.

Star bowl

This bowl is an old copper one I bought very cheaply from a junk shop. It is decorated using the dribbling technique and non-waterbased ceramic paints. The original copper shows through the paint here and there to give an interesting effect. Stencilled stars add the finishing touch (see page 301).

Leaf bowl

This uses the same technique as the star and fleur de lys bowls, but white is added to the paint to create pastel shades (see page 301 for the pattern).

Fish bowl

Blue and green non-waterbased ceramic paints are used with the dribbling technique (see pages 296–297) to create the watery-looking background on this bowl. This is allowed to dry for twenty-four hours before the designs are transferred on to the side of the bowl using carbon paper and the patterns provided. The fish are painted and left to dry. The detailing on the fins and scales is then added using gold paint decanted into a plastic bottle fitted with a 0.5mm metal nozzle. Finally, the rim is sponged with gold paint.

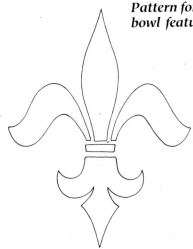

Pattern for the fleur de lys bowl featured on page 298

Pattern for the leaf bowl featured on page 299

Pattern for the star bowl featured on page 299

Patterns for the fish bowl opposite

INDEX

First published in Great Britain 1999

Search Press Limited
Wellwood, North Farm Road,
Tunbridge Wells, Kent TN2 3DR

Reprinted 2000, 2001

Originally published as five separate titles:
Paint Effects by Lindsey Durrant
Decorative Painting by Sandy Barnes
Restyling Junk by Jane Gordon-Smith
Decorative Stamping for the Home by Michelle Powell
Decorative Painting on Glass, Ceramics & Metal by Judy Balchin

ISBN 0 85532 905 X

The Publishers and author can accept no responsibility for any consequences arising from the information, advice or instructions given in this publication.

Readers are permitted to reproduce any of the items/patterns in this book for their personal use, or for the purposes of selling for charity, free of charge and without the prior permission of the Publishers. Any use of the items/patterns for commercial purposes is not permitted without the prior permission of the Publishers.

Suppliers

If you have difficulty in obtaining any of the materials and equipment mentioned in this book, then please write to the Publishers, at the address above, for a current list of stockists, including firms who operate a mail-order service.

The Publishers would like to thank the following for providing many of the materials used in this book: Craig and Rose Plc., 172 Leith Walk, Edinburgh, EH6 5EV; Pebeo UK Ltd., Unit 109, Solent Business Centre, Millbrook, Southampton, SO15 0HW; ColArt, Whitefriars Avenue, Wealdstone, Harrow, Middlesex, HH3 5RH; and Thomas Seth & Co. Ltd., Tomas Seth Business Park, Argent Road, Queenborough, Sheppey, Kent, ME11 5JP.

Thanks also to Sue Goodhand for supplying the majority of the wooden items that have been painted by Sandy Barnes. A mail order catalogue can be obtained from Goodhands Decorative Folk Art, 1 Bentley Close, Horndean, Waterlooville, Hants, PO8 9HH.

Thank you to Crowson Fabrics Ltd., Bellbrook Park, Uckfield, East Sussex, TN22 1QZ for supplying the fabric which is used as the basis for the homemade stamp featured on pages 118–119.

Thanks to the National Gallery Publications Ltd., Trafalgar Square, London, WC2N 5DN; Mamelok Press Limited, Northern Way, Bury St Edmunds, Suffolk, IP32 6NJ; and Woodmansterne Publications Ltd., 1 The Boulevard, Blackmoor Lane, Watford, Hertfordshire, WD1 8YW for their kind permission to use the majority of the giftwrap images featured in this book.

With thanks also to Fenwick Limited, Royal Victoria Place, Tunbridge Wells, Kent, TN1 2SR for providing some of the props for photography.

Colour separation by P&W Graphics, Singapore
Printed by Times Offset, Malaysia

Publishers' note

All the step-by-step photographs in this book feature the authors demonstrating how to create decorative effects for the home. No models have been used.

Colour Conversion Chart

Jo Sonja Artists	Accent	Deco Art Americana	Delta Ceram Coat	Liquitex
Aqua	Marina Blue	Desert Turquoise	Laguna	Turquoise
Brown Earth	Burnt Sienna +/-	Fudge + Santa Red	Burnt Umber	Burnt Umber
Brilliant Green	Holiday Green	Bright Green	Jubilee Green	Perm Grn Lt
Burgundy	Burgundy Wine	Mendocino	Cranberry	Dp Brilliant Red
Burnt Sienna	Burnt Sienna	Burnt Sienna	Burnt Sienna	Burnt Sienna
Carbon Black	Soft + Real Black	Ebony	Black	Ivory Black
Dioxide Purple	True Purple	Diox Purple	Purple	Diox Purple
Fawn	Wicker + Choc Mse	Sable Brown	Bambi	Sandlewood
Gold Oxide	Sedona Clay	Terra Cotta	Mexicana	Raw S + Red Oxide
Green Oxide	Gr Olive + Gr Apple	Mistletoe	Chrome Green Lt	Chrome Ox Gr
Indian Red Oxide	Fingerberry Red	Rockwood Red	Candy Bar	B Umber + Nap Cr
Moss Green	Chat Moss + Gld Hvt	Olive + Sable Br	Olive Yellow	Hooker Grn + Flax
Napthol Crimson	Jo Sonja Red +/-	Calico Red	Napthol Crimson	Alizarine Crimson
Napthol Red Light	Jo Sonja Red +/-	Berry Red	Napthol Red Lt	Napthol Red Lt
Nimbus Grey	Soft Gray + Wicker	Slate + Mink	Cadet Grey	Neutral Grey #7
Norwegian Orange	Sedona Clay + JS Red	Burnt O + Cash Red	G Clay + Nap R Lt	Opal Lt Pch N Cr + V
Opal	Lt PNC + V Mve + Wt	Flesh + Cash Beige	Dresden Flesh	Un Titan + Lt Por Pnk
Payne's Grey	Soldier Blue +/-	Uniform Blue	Midnight	Payne's Grey
Pine Green	Pn Ndl Gr + Pr Ye	Avocado	Dark Jungle	Hooker Grn + Y O
Provincial Beige	Raw Sienna + White	Sable Brown	Territorial Beige	Sandlewd + Bu + T Y
Prussian Blue Hue	Windsor Blue	Navy Blue	Prussian Blue	Pthalo Blue + Blk
Pthalo Blue	Ultramarine Blue +/-	True Blue	Manganese Blue	Pthalo Blue
Raw Sienna	Mustard Seed	Terra Cotta + Fudge	Raw Sienna	Raw Sienna
Raw Umber	Real Umber	Dk Chocolate	Raw Umber	Raw Umber
Red Earth	Pennsylvania Clay	Rustee + Bnt Sienna	Red Iron Oxide	Red Oxide
Rich gold	King's Gold +/-	Venetian Gold	Kim Gold	Gold - Met.
Rose Pink	Holiday Red + Cl Rse	Santa + Gooseberry	Rouge	Acra Red
Sapphire	Windsor Bl + Larkspur	Victorian Blue	Liberty Blue	Cerulean Blue
Smoked Pearl	Off Wht + Wld Honey	Antique White	Sandstone	Un Ti + Mars Blk
Storm Blue	Liberty Blue	Navy + Black	Dk Night + Avalon	Ultra Bl + Bnt Umber
Teal Green	Telemark Green	Bluegrass + Black	Deep River	Hooker's Green
Transparent Magenta	H Rd + Pt Dsrt + Tr Prp	Burgundy Wine	Sweetheart Blush	Med Magenta
Turner's Yellow	Dijon Gold	Honey Toast	Empire Gold	Turner's Yellow
Ultramarine	Pure Blue	True Blue	Ultra Blue	Ultramarine
Vermillion	True Orange	Cad O + Tangerine	Tangerine	Scarlet Red + B Yel
Yellow Light	Pure Yellow	Lemon Yellow	Bright Yellow	Bright Yellow
Yellow Oxide	Golden Harvest	Antique Gold	Antique Gold	Harvest Gold
Warm White	White + Adobe Wsh	Buttermilk	Antique White	White + Parchment

Get creative with **Search Press**

- A huge selection of art and craft books, available from all good book shops and art and craft suppliers
- Clear instructions, many in step-by-step format
- All projects are tried and tested
- Full colour throughout

If you are interested in any books published by Search Press, please send for a free catalogue to:

SEARCH PRESS LTD., Department B, Wellwood, North Farm Road, Tunbridge Wells, Kent TN2 3DR
Tel: (01892) 510850   *Fax:* (01892) 515903   *E-mail:* sales@searchpress.com

or (if resident in the USA) to:

ARTHUR SCWARTZ & CO. INC., 234 Meads Mountain Road, Woodstock, NY 12498
Tel: (914) 679 4024   *Fax:* (914) 679 4093
Orders, toll free: 800 669 9080

- Perfect for the enthusiast and the specialist alike
- Free colour catalogue
- Friendly, fast, efficient service
- Customers come back to us again and again